BACK FROM THE BRINK

BACK FROM THE BRINK

Saying No to Suicide

Chris F. Minshew

Introduction By
Mardi Allen, Ph.D.

SARTORIS
LITERARY
GROUP

A traditional publisher
with a non-traditional approach to publishing

SARTORIS LITERARY GROUP
www.sartorisliterary.com

This book is dedicated to those who courageously shared the most painful moment of their life so that others may understand the struggle of suicide from the inside. You are not alone.

"There is power in the personal narrative. *Back From The Brink* is an intimate collection of stories provided by individuals who've survived attempting suicide. This unique book gives a voice to a pervasive epidemic so many struggle to talk about. These are stories that need to be heard."—**J.L. Craig, Ph.D., Clinical Psychologist**

"Who knows more about suicide than someone who has attempted it , or changed their mind at the last minute, and gone on to live a productive life? Chris F. Minshew has done a public service by interviewing individuals who have attempted suicide and recovered, or who have journeyed to the brink of suicide and stepped back to say no to taking their own lives, himself included. Their stories of struggle and redemption are inspirational. This is an excellent book for anyone who is contemplating suicide because it shows there is always hope."—**Kris Jones, MSW, Project Director, SAMSHA Suicide Prevention grant**

"Through this compilation of the exceptional and courageous stories of those who have faced suicide, Chris Minshew provides a unique view into the agonizing struggle when one comes to the point of unbearable life. The personal chronicles of those who have survived suicide are both touching and disturbing as they tap into the struggles for the reader who relates to this overwhelming experience. This book will validate the sorrow of suicide, yet will offer hope for the return to life."—**James D. Herzog, Ph.D., Clinical Psychologist**

"Chris has taken a subject that people only speak about in hushed tones of embarrassment, or do not speak about at all. But the topic of suicide should be spoken about for all to hear because it affects many people. Back From The Brink brings this topic out of the darkest places of our soul and sheds light on it to let us all know, we are not alone in our scariest moments of loneliness and pain. I applaud Chris for writing an honest truth about a taboo subject. Bringing it out in the open will save lives."—**Jamie Roth, author of The General Manager Of Your Universe**

CONTENTS

BACK FROM THE BRINK

INTRODUCTION
By Mardi Allen, Ph.D.

The word suicide evokes emotions, creates uneasiness, and elicits memories of those we love who have tarried at the brink and made that crucial decision to choose life or death. Suicide has become pervasive in our society. Whether they are spouses, family members, friends, or co-workers, someone we know has considered, attempted or committed suicide.

The overwhelming majority of those who consider or attempt suicide claim they never really wanted to die, but had lost hope and believed they had no options for a better life. The pain of living seemed to outweigh the decision to die at that moment. Most who commit suicide are not particularly different or exhibit bizarre behaviors. For the most part, they walk among us, suffering in silence.

This book is a collection of true stories told by individuals who have walked to the edge of death, some finding the strength to turn away and choose life—and others actually surviving their own attempt to cause death by suicide. The stories are different in details, but similar in their recognition of having the compelling thought that death was their only option at the time.

Readers will empathize with the pain of broken lives and feel the scuffle some encounter to regain power over their destiny. The individuals telling their stories all have opened deep wounds to share; none regret not dying, but many confess their continuing battles against personal demons. We are grateful to the book contributors for their courage to share their story in hopes of making a difference.

The narratives help readers understand the personal circumstances that lead the individual to make a deadly decision and what changed their mind. The book also provides a brief overview of current suicide statistics, research findings and recommendations for early identification and intervention.

When suicide strikes, those affected recall recent interactions with the individual. "Were there clues, could I have changed things?" we ask. Typically when an individual is contemplating suicide, he assumes his thoughts and plans are private and no one will know until it's done. However, there are usually specific signs and symptoms, yet they go unrecognized as current predictors.

In his book *Melissa: A Father's Lessons from a Daughter's Suicide*, Dr. Frank Page shares his years of despair as he tried to sort out what he missed, how he could have helped his daughter or what he did wrong that allowed her to resort to killing herself. He describes his daughter as having years of ups and downs, but he can't resolve why this time was different and she chose death. Sadly, the person gone made the deadly decision having falsely assumed that they know best for all involved.

The reality is that all of us are capable of ending our life. Most of us have thought of it least once. The good news is that it usually stops as a passing thought, never to be acted on. Anyone can be at risk. Society is relatively unaware that a large cross-section of citizens constantly teeter on the brink of suicide. The agonizing screams of a teenager over a breakup, vowing she has no reason to live, is easily recognized as high risk. School officials, parents and friends have learned to take such threats seriously.

But unfortunately, it is the quiet, unassuming individual who withdraws in times of adversity, or the loud, boisterous one who seems to thrive on attention that shocks us when death became their a choice.

Most of us are fairly resilient and bounce back when bad things happen, but when emotional vulnerability fortuitously clashes with a loss of hope, thoughts of suicide become a dangerous option.

Suicide is not limited by demographics, by class, race, income, education, age or profession. There are surveillance data that offer clues to increased risk; but no group is considered immune. Each suicide is an individual tragedy that didn't have to occur.

Resilience has been found to play a crucial role in risk and recovery. As a therapist I have used an analogy of a beautiful tapestry to represent our life. There are threads of the tapestry crucial to providing strength, whereas other threads add color and beautiful elegance to the work of art. Our personal tapestry of life is being woven constantly, waxing and waning as happy and sad events occur, diseases, fortune and hardships come our way.

We are all vulnerable humans and often our outcomes are a matter of timing. In reflection, we can identify times in our life when bouncing back, or seeing a light at the end of the tunnel, wasn't easy. Maybe you have weathered hardships and disease, but with resilience found your way through it. Your life tapestry has a few holes and weak spots, but there was enough strength to keep it intact. Society falsely assumes that those who were once strong are always strong. That isn't the case.

Most suicide attempts are associated with adverse life events. Bad things happen, that's a given, but how one typically handles life's problems can be telling. Our personality, experiences and environment influence our responses from a happy go lucky attitude that brushes off any adversity to a troubled worrier.

An individual's vulnerability can vary through life. Typically, past behaviors are the best predictor of current and future behaviors. That being said, factors such as the severity and number of adversities hinder one's coping behaviors. Pain, hardship and suffering can build resilience, but the cumulative affect can render one defenseless. Even minor problems in large numbers can interfere with resiliency.

Emotional challenges deplete one's ability to think clearly and use well-developed coping skills. As problems mount in tandem with anxiety, depression or other emotional challenges, a downward spiral is likely. Once an individual has fallen into the dark hole of hopelessness, it becomes very difficult to feel confident in your ability to solve even minor problems. Family and friends may not recognize that this time is different. They may assume their loved one will muscle through as they always have and may succumb to their own anxiety and feel inadequate to intervene in another's life. Tragedy can occur when we don't ask for help or when we don't know to intervene.

In his book, *Cracked but not Broken*, Kevin Hines, one of the few individuals who has survived jumping off the San Francisco Golden Gate Bridge, describes making a deal with himself on the day of his attempt. He told himself that if anyone acknowledged his pain, or asked if he was suicidal, or otherwise let him know they understood what he was feeling, then he would interpret that as a sliver of hope and not jump.

He didn't really want to die; he just wanted the pain to stop.

His dad asked him to go to his office with him that morning. It was a nice gesture, but not what he was looking for. The staffer in the dean's office said, "We will miss you" when he dropped all of his classes except the one with the attractive professor.

Another failed test.

The city bus driver who looked at him crying in the back of the bus as they sat at the bridge, the last stop on the route, and said, "Last stop, you need to get off."

Couldn't he have least asked why he was crying? The message was clear: Fate wanted him to die.

As he stood crying on the bridge, a pretty tourist approached. He looked up with anticipation and hope as she calmly reached out to him, handing him her camera. She asked if he would take her picture. He describes glimmers of hope, but none really came.

The handwriting was on the wall.

He jumped.

At the very moment his fall began, he knew it was a mistake and he should never have jumped. Kevin survived, but not without severe physical and emotional damage. He continues to deal with a long history mental illness and suicidal thoughts, but his support system is vigilant and is proactive when needed.

When people are contemplating death or continuing life, they usually fall into faulty thinking. They believe no one can understand their pain and that the situation is so catastrophic that there is no resolution possible.

On the day Kevin jumped, he was personally paralyzed with pain and put his life in the hands of others. He wanted someone to say the exact words he needed to hear to not proceed with his jump.

Kevin had given up on himself and tried to bargain with God by laying his fate at the feet of strangers. Of course, if anyone who crossed his path had known his emotional state they would have said the words he was looking for. His father tried that morning, but Kevin was discarding any broad attempt while looking for an exact script he had decided to bet his life on.

What increases choosing life over death? As you read these stories, focus on the person, his pain, his situation and environment. There are many lessons to be learned in stories of those who came back from the brink and said no to suicide.

Mardi Allen, Ph.D. is a psychologist with many years experience and co-author of *How to Screen Adoptive and Foster Parents* and *Sons Without Fathers: What Every Mother Needs to Know.*

Tell Me
When I Am At The Brink

18

1

Desperate Housewife

As a child, I was always taught that suicide is wrong.

That's easy to accept when, as a kid, you have no bills, no stress, and no responsibilities. When you're a middle-aged housewife with two kids, a husband who is terrible with finances, and a mound of overdue bills, it starts looking pretty damned good.

My childhood was nothing special. I grew up in a typical suburban American household. Even though we weren't "well off," I never wanted for the essentials. Sure, there were things I thought were essential that I didn't get, like new shoes and new clothes. But, all-in-all, things were all right.

If my parents ever fought about finances or anything else, it was so underwhelming that my brother and I never noticed. That's why my current situation became so hard to deal with. Things had gotten so bad financially that we were in arrears on every bill in the house.

My husband's way of dealing with problems is to ignore them. If you don't talk about them, they go away. I wish it were that simple.

Well, one night we were laying in bed when all of a sudden I heard my car door and then the sound of it cranking. I looked at my husband and screamed "somebody's stealing my car!"

But he just laid there. It was the oddest thing.

He just looked at me with this peculiar sense of shame in his eyes. It's like he wasn't concerned. That wasn't it at all, though. Finally, he said, "Your car wasn't stolen—it just got repossessed."

Oh my God! That was the first undeniable bit of proof I had that we were in deep trouble. There's no way he could ignore this any longer. We stayed up for hours crying, screaming, and even laughing.

Through all the pain and heartache we were experiencing, we actually had a few good moments mixed in talking about things we had done and trips we had taken with the kids when they were still young. It's like once we started talking, it just opened up a floodgate of emotions we had both been keeping bottled up.

If only that were the end of the story. Not even close.

Sure, we buckled down on all of our spending for a while. Any money that came in went toward the most overdue bills with the highest interest first. We moved down the line of bills until there was no more money left to divide. (There were always more bills than money.)

We cruised along like that for a few months, scraping along little by little.

Then the unthinkable happened. I got hurt on the job. That's normally not a huge deal because worker's compensation generally will help you until you're able to return to work. Not in my state! We have worker's comp here, but in our state you can lose your job after being injured (even after filing worker's comp). The injury was not career-ending by any means either.

Basically, I dislocated my shoulder doing what was routine work on the assembly line. I slipped on a wet floor mat and went to catch myself as I fell. The way I grabbed the nearest rail on my way down made my shoulder come out of place. It made one hell of a pop when it happened, too. It was pretty gross, to tell you the truth. But, like I said, a few weeks of rest and rehab is all I really needed and I'd be as good as new.

While in the "waiting" period between when I filed my worker's comp claim and the time I was supposed to hear about it, I got a certified letter from my company. I thought, "Wow, this got pushed through a lot quicker than I expected."

Unfortunately, it was from the legal department of my company. It said in a roundabout, legal mumbo-jumbo kind of way that I was no longer needed because of "downsizing."

The last sentence did say that since I was no longer employed with them, my worker's comp claim had been denied. What the hell happened? That is so twisted. I worked hard every week. I never took a sick day and rarely took vacation (mainly because we could never afford to go anywhere). So, when I have a legitimate accident in the workplace, I get fired for it! That's gratitude for you.

Then it hit me. What was my husband going to say? He would be home from work in a couple of hours. How would I even tell him? This was going to throw a major monkey wrench in our meager budget without a doubt. A million things raced through my mind. At the forefront were all the ways I could make money, legal or not. I'm not proud of it, but in times of extreme distress, sometimes extreme solutions are necessary.

My mind first flashed back to all the jobs I had prior to this one. I had done everything from cutting yards to exotic dancing. Yes, stripping. If only I had the body I did twenty years ago, I'd be back in the club in a heartbeat. That was not the most glamorous job, but the money is insane. On a good night, I made over a thousand dollars, cash. And there were a lot of good nights back then. Needless to say, that was absolutely out of the question.

While I was in the middle of my trip down memory lane, I heard my husband's truck coming up the driveway. Oh shit. He came in and threw his toolbox down. Holy crap, this is not going to be easy. I asked him what was wrong. He said, "Same old shit, different day." I knew well enough what that meant. His supervisor is about fifteen years younger than my husband and thinks he's God's gift to the world. Typical pencil-pushing geek fresh out of college. This was going to be much harder than I anticipated.

Luckily, I had prepared a "heavy" dish for supper. Something that sits heavy on you after you eat it. Tonight it was chicken alfredo, heavy on the sauce. Usually after eating one of my "heavy" meals, my husband makes his way over to the recliner, puts the television on the sports channel and starts dozing off in less than thirty minutes. I was hoping tonight wasn't much different. I waited for him to finish eating and get in his recliner before breaking the news.

The meal had absolutely no effect on his reaction. When I told him about the certified letter he screamed at the top of his lungs, "Fuck those pencil-pushing bastards!" Then he began yelling at me about why did I have to get hurt. Didn't I know all the safety procedures and why was I so clumsy? How the hell did this become my fault all of a sudden?

I knew he'd be mad, I just didn't expect for it to be at me. After twenty-five years of marriage, didn't he know me well enough to know that I always put our family first? Why would I jeopardize our family's well-being by getting hurt on purpose? Up until this accident, I had actually been awarded for my stellar safety record. He had absolutley lost his mind. I guess that was the final straw for him and he couldn't contain his frustration any longer. But I still can't believe he turned on me. After all this time together, the sense of betrayal and utter loneliness was beyond comprehension.

I walked out of the living room and left him in his recliner to calm down. I was far from calm, though. The further I got from him, the more furious I got. How in the hell could he think it was my fault for being careless? It's as if he thinks I did it on purpose so I could stay at home and twiddle my thumbs. Son of a bitch!

I went to the bedroom and got the pistol from the night stand on my husband's side of the bed. I'm not sure what kind or size it was, but I damn sure knew it was loaded.

"What good is an unloaded gun?" he always said.

He was about to find out what I could do with it. I stuck it in my back pocket, stormed back through the living room into the kitchen, and kicked open the door to the carport without breaking stride. From there, I went straight toward the barn. That was my safe place, where I would go when I wanted to be alone.

Tonight it was going to have a very different role. It would be the place my husband would find me dead. I was going out there to end it all. No more bills, no more money problems, no more bullshit.

When I got outside, all I could hear was the sound of crickets and bullfrogs. Since we live away from town, the "night" animals are usually all you hear when you walk outside. Maybe my senses were heightened because tonight the sound was almost deafening. By the time I got to the barn, I had noticed my gait was a little slower and lighter.

Subconsciously, I had been so focused on the sounds of the night that I had started calming down. I found a bucket, turned it over, and sat down. The smell of nature can be quite beautiful as well. One by one, I tried to identify the various smells in the air (hay bales, roses, a skunk). As I leaned back to prop against the barn wall, I felt the pressure of the gun in my back pocket and was instantly brought back to reality.

The whole reason I came out there was to kill myself. Instead, I was reminded about all the beautiful things that exist whether we're there to enjoy them or not. That was quite an eye-opening realization. If I killed myself, the sound of the gun would disturb the crickets and the frogs . . . for a few seconds. Then they'd go right back to doing what they do. No matter whether I existed or not, the world would keep turning and the birds would keep chirping.

With that, I took a few deep breaths of that refreshing country air and slowly walked back to the house. When I got back in the kitchen, my husband was sitting at the table still fuming. I reached in my back pocket and pulled out the pistol. The look on his face changed dramatically.

Was that a hint of fear I detected? I believe for a split second he thought I was going to kill him. Instead, I dropped the pistol on the table, turned, and walked to the bedroom, without ever uttering a word. I got in the bed and went to sleep within seconds. It may have been the single greatest night of sleep I've ever had. I'm not sure when my husband came to bed, but I'm guessing he was careful not to wake me.

The next morning, by the time I had awakened, he had already gone to work. On the kitchen table was a note from him. It said, "I love you so much. We will get through this, come hell or high water. This too shall pass." For the first time in quite a while, I had a genuine smile on my face.

It's been two years since that night I kicked open the kitchen door on my way to kill myself. I have since found another job. The pay is pretty much equivalent to the last one. Financially, things are about the same as they were before, too, with one exception. We don't fight about the bills anymore. Sure, they come up, but we talk it out like two rational adults and stick as close to our budget as we can.

Things have never gotten as bad as they did that one night. Mainly because of my attitude about things. Having children, I have to remember, is what my life is about right now. No matter how bad I think my life is, it's *their* time now. Mine will come soon enough. Whenever I get downhearted and start feeling tense, I open the kitchen door (with my hand, not my foot), calmly stroll to the barn, flip over a bucket, and take in all the beauty that nature has to offer. The sound of the crickets and the bullfrogs is a constant reminder that "this too shall pass."

2

Accidential Junkie

My life has been quite the comedy of errors. The bulk of my problems began at age fourteen. My parents were both raging alcoholics. Are there any other kind? My mother was the oldest of thirteen siblings. As the oldest, it was her job to help her parents raise all the other kids. By the time she was sixteen, she was married.

I think it was just so she could get away from her family and the job of raising her siblings. It didn't take my mom long for her to get tired of raising her daughter, too. At fourteen, my mother handed me off to our neighbors. She said they could raise me because she didn't want to do it anymore. In a rural community like where I grew up, your neighbors helped you out in a pinch, but there *is* a limit. After six months, I moved in with my aunt. A few months after that, I was shipped off to my grandparents.

That's when things went from bad to worse. My grandfather was a severe alcoholic. And when he got into the worst of his alcoholic rages, he would touch me inappropriately (at first). After a few times, he began trying to forcibly have sex with me, but I was always able to fight him off.

One night, however, he made up his mind it was going to happen. He locked all the windows and doors and began forcing himself on me yet again. This time I couldn't run out the front door as I had before. But I could run from room to room. Finally, all the physical activity of chasing me and fighting with me got to him and he had to lay down on the couch to rest.

While he was resting, I went to the kitchen and got his pills off the top of the refrigerator. I don't know what they were, just that they were what he'd take when he was upset. Well, I was damn upset. The bottle was mostly full and I took every last one of those pills.

The next thing I knew, my uncle was shaking me violently, trying to get me to wake up. He lived next door and must've heard the commotion of my grandfather and me fighting. While I was passed out on the floor, he had come over and kicked the front door in. That's when he found me on the floor, nearly dead.

He picked me up and took me to his house to recover. They weren't the kind that really believed in hospitals. It was all home-remedies in our little slice of heaven. My aunt whipped up something that made me wish I was dead. Withing minutes of drinking it, I was basically projectile-vomiting everything in my stomach, like the girl in that horror movie spewing split pea soup! Any trace of pills (or anything else for that matter) were definitely no longer in my system.

Things went well for the next few weeks, until the same uncle that had come to my rescue that fateful night began doing the same thing to me as my grandfather. Is there anyone in my family that's not a child-molesting rapist? That sent me into a pattern of self-destructive behavior that became my only way to escape the storm I lived in constantly.

Oh, sure, at first I took a few pills to help me sleep. Then I took a few to help me get going in the morning. It didn't take long for me to quit fooling myself and just take them because I enjoyed it. No reason necessary. It was at that point that I was a full-blown addict. The pills made all the hurt and the disappointment disappear, until they wore off. Then it was time to take more. The main thing I wanted was to not feel anything (good, bad, or indifferent).

After a few years of self-destruction, I found a man that shared the same taste for pills as me. And he liked me! It didn't take long for us to move in together. It wasn't long after that until we were married. I just needed something I could depend on, you know? Marriage seemed to be it, for a while.

It didn't take long for that to turn sour as well. Why the hell did everyone I care about turn out to be such assholes? After we got married, my husband beat me every day we were together. Every day. I guess at that point he felt like I was his legal property with which he could do as he pleased. It was the same pattern as before with my grandfather and my uncle. The person I lived with who was supposed to love and protect me ended up being my jailor.

After a couple of years of marriage, I got pregnant and had a beautiful child. At least, that's what I was told. I stayed high all the time, I barely remember the pregnancy or the delivery. Only a few months after that, I was arrested for my fourth DWI (driving while intoxicated). That's a serious one.

I was sentenced to a fifteen-year prison term, with a minimum incarceration time of seven years. Little did I know at the time, however, that was going to be my ultimate saving grace. It was in prison that I found the will to live, without pills or any other artificial stimulants. I'm not going to pretend and say the second I walked through the prison doors, the clouds parted and I heard angels singing.

That first week, I prayed for death. Suicide was just about the only thing I could think of that whole time. I wanted to die so I didn't have to endure that hell hole or the consequences of my actions. That's the funny thing, though. I *prayed* for death. That was the first time I had actually prayed for anything since I was a little girl praying for a specific Christmas gift (which I didn't get). The journey of a thousand steps begins with the first one, right? That prayer for death was the beginning of my thousand-step journey.

After the first few nights of praying for death, I began adding things like safety, peace, and comfort. Eventually,

I didn't even mention death anymore. Also, I began noticing how much better I would sleep after I prayed. Maybe there's something to this whole prayer crap after all.

After a year in lockup, I had a backslide moment. One of my friends on the outside I hadn't seen since I went to jail came to visit me. She smuggled a few pills in to me. To her, it was a nice gesture. To me, it was a potential ticket to solitary confinement. Despite my better judgment, I took them back with me to my cell.

Before I could take them, a guard showed up at my cell and dragged me off to the warden's office. My heart was pounding and I was expecting the worst. When the warden walked in, the first thing that caught my attention was when she called me by my name, not my number. That may not sound like much, but in the prison world, that is huge. They use numbers to keep you as inventory, not human.

She said she had been watching me closely the last few months and had noticed my change in demeanor and how the other inmates tended to come to me when they had problems. I guess they really do pay more attention than I thought. She said she had also noticed that I accepted pills smuggled in by a visitor and took them back to my cell. (My friend was arrested before she ever got halfway out of the visitors' area.) That's when I expected the hammer to drop on me.

Instead, she said, "Do you want to live or die?"

I said "live."

"You're sure not acting like it," she said. "Why are you willing to throw away the example you've been setting for all the other inmates by doing something so stupid as take a few pills someone smuggled in to you . . . in their ass?"

That unfettered, and downright gross, visualization was just what I needed to help me see how big of a mistake I was about to make, for a quick, cheap thrill.

It was at that point when I found out just how great a woman our warden was. She began witnessing to me about the hard times she had endured in her life (including an abusive husband at one point). She was such a strong, self-assured person. I couldn't imagine her ever letting a man talk down to her, much less physically abuse her.

That was part of her point to me. It was up to me to change, no one else. She told me to take this little slip up as the lesson it is and make a promise to her and myself that I would never succumb to temptation like that again.

I swore on my life. If it hadn't been for this very Godly and compassionate warden who took me under her wing and mentored me, I would have ended up as just another statistic. From that point on, I enrolled in every class and positive extra-curricular activity our prison had to offer. She also encouraged me to work my way up through the kitchen, then on to laundry, and eventually working for her as her personal secretary. She did all this by treating me as a human being, not just another animal in her "zoo." Turns out, she wasn't such a cast-iron bitch after all.

It's amazing how quickly time can move when you're doing the right thing and not worrying about if you're going to get "caught" doing something you shouldn't. That's how the rest of my time in prison went. I became a mentor to as many of my fellow inmates as would ask me. So many of them began calling me "mom," either because they hated their own mother or never even knew her. It was a bittersweet role for me as well. On the outside, my child was being raised without a mother. I guess this was my way of coping with not being able to raise my own child. If I could help my fellow inmates who had "mommy" issues get past them, maybe someone on the outside was helping mine too.

After my time had been served, I have to admit I was a little sad to be released. That's how it is in life, once you get comfortable in a certain setting, you don't want any more change, even if that means staying in prison as opposed to getting out.

Once I got out, I kept in close contact with the warden as well as the other inmates I had befriended and mentored. I didn't want to be like so many of the other inmates that I had known who said they'd keep in touch once they got out but disappeared like a ghost. I can't say I blame them, though. Prison is a hard life that most people want to put behind them and forget. I never want to forget. Because that's the place that saved my life.

The reason I'm sharing my story is because I want others to know that when you think it's about to end, it's most likely just the beginning. Eventually, the meaning of it all will be revealed to you. So many times, I should have died, but I didn't. It was for a reason, and I know it's because of God.

Here's a perfect example. A year before I went to prison, I ran off the road into a ditch filled with water. Of course, I was high on pills. The car had flipped upside down and the car was filling with water, fast. I was trapped by the seatbelt and couldn't get out. I just knew I was about to drown.

Then a man in a long, black trench coat approached the door of my car and pulled it open. He cut my seatbelt, dragged me out of the car, and pulled me up the embankment out of harm's way.

When I awoke, the paramedics were working on me. I asked them where the man was that helped me. I told them what happened. They said, "Ma'am, there's no one around here, just you. Plus, your seatbelt was not cut."

Tell me the Lord doesn't work miracles! He could have easily let me die that day and I would've been just another junkie that died in a car wreck. I was saved so I could go to prison a year later and transform into the person I am today. Some people would have rather died than gone to prison. Not me. Prison is not the end of the road, it's just a fork.

3

Banker

I knew I was going to jail in a few days. My ex-wife said she would never allow our kids to see me in jail . . . no way, no how. The lady I was dating at the time said she was going to break up with me because she didn't want to be dating a "jailbird."

You might say things weren't all roses and sunshine for me at that point in my life.

Having spent a significant portion of my life in the banking industry, I had gotten sick of being financially strapped. I mean, I was surrounded by money day in and day out. It was quite disparaging to be in charge of other people's money when I could barely keep enough in my account for the basic staples of life. I don't know if it was calculated or if it was more of a comedy of errors, but one day it just dawned on me: Why not skim a little off of other people's accounts. If I spread it around enough, no one would even notice (especially the largest accounts). And so it began.

I started out with a little here and a little there. That went on for a few months. I couldn't believe how easy this was. That's when the downward spiral really started. The ego kicked in and I started getting careless. Needless to say, my actions triggered some red flags. Little did I know that the last few months of my activities were being heavily monitored.

The authorities were giving me all the rope I needed to hang myself. They were just sitting back, waiting for the right time to tighten the noose. It's funny how arrogance, ego, and greed can take down the mightiest of men. I was so blinded by my "accomplishments" that I didn't stop to think how it looked to everyone around me that I was wearing nicer clothes, eating out more often, and driving a better car, without any kind of significant raise or a promotion. Ego.

When the authorities felt like they had enough evidence for an open-and-shut case, they sprung the trap on me. The court trial was merely a formality. When I saw what all they had against me, I pleaded guilty and made a deal. There was no lawyer in the world that could have gotten me out of this conviction (at least not one that I could afford). Swiftly and judiciously, I was handed a felony conviction for embezzlement with a sentence of six years in prison. For those of you who don't know much about these types of things, a felony conviction stays with you forever. It's like a bad STD that keeps popping up at the most inopportune moments.

You can forget ever getting a "professional" job. Get comfortable with hourly compensation and work shirts with your name stitched on it. If you like to hunt or just like owning a gun for your own personal protection, forget that too. However, there is the possibility of getting your record expunged so the felony conviction "disappears" but you have to have one hell of an attorney and an inside connection with the current governor. Not an option for me!

As I said before, I knew I was going to jail in less than a week. That was NOT going to happen. I know I did wrong and was justly convicted. However, that didn't mean I had to actually go to jail, not if I could help it.

The plan was simple, I had researched it and knew exactly what I wanted to do. The thought of blowing my brains out was just too gruesome of an image for me. It was so nasty and, honestly, quite inconsiderate for those who had to clean up the mess. I didn't want a bunch of folks gathered around my body cursing at me while they bagged and tagged everything. I preferred they found me "asleep" in my car. That's why I chose to take a bunch of pills. It would be a simple (and clean) way to just slip on over to the other side. Quite brilliant, actually.

So, the day was here. As I gathered up all the pills in my apartment, I have to admit, I was pretty exhilarated. I would certainly get the last laugh. Yes, I did the crime. Yes, I got caught. But, no, I was not going to jail. What I had in mind was I would get in my car, go through a drive-thru (a man's gotta eat), and find a nice, peaceful place to park. People put so much emphasis on your "last meal." That part for me was more of an impulse. I mean, who really knows what they're going to want to eat the day they're going to die?

As I pulled out of the parking lot, I let my stomach guide me. Pizza? No, that would take too long. Tacos? No, I don't want my last sensation to be heartburn. Burgers? Yes! Just a couple of miles away was my favorite burger joint. Perfect! As I approached the drive-thru I was definitely not thinking about calories. When I finished placing my order the lady asked, "Would you like to super-size that?" I said, "Yes, yes I would..." Why the hell not, right? The most peculiar part of it was I still ordered a diet drink. Old habits die hard, I guess.

Now I just had to find the perfect location to relax, eat my meal, and stage my final departure. It was actually a very pleasant day. Slightly overcast, with a moderate temperature. In the distance, I could see the spot. In the edge of the parking lot of my favorite mega-store was a beautiful, old oak tree. It was quite majestic. Now that's the place where a man can enjoy a good meal and take a long, peaceful nap. I pulled in and parked in the spot closest to the tree. There was plenty of shade and there wasn't another car within 100 or more feet. Perfect.

I don't know if my senses were overly heightened from the thought of what was to come or if I was just terribly hungry, but that was, without a doubt, the best hamburger I had ever eaten in my entire life! So now the time had come. I opened the plastic bag with all the pill bottles in it. There were so many to choose from, why not take some of all?

So I did. A handful of Tylenol PM. A handful of Tylenol 3. A handful of Extra Strenght Tylenol. There must have been over 30 pills in me before I was done. As I was waiting for the pills to kick in, it was now time to execute the final step of my plan. I typed up an email on my phone explaining what I had just done, why I had done it, and hit "send."

The recipients were the people I thought might care to know. My mom, my ex-wife (she'd be thrilled, I know), my (soon-to-be ex) girlfriend, and my three children. I grabbed the newspaper in the passenger's seat and began flipping through it. My phone immediately began blowing up with texts and phone calls.

I had said everything to them I cared to say. Why wouldn't they just let me be? So, I ignored them as long as I could. Finally, I answered one of the calls. It was my ex-wife. She pleaded with me to tell her where I was. Using the idea of how bad our kids would be hurt by this, she pried the town out of me. I still wouldn't give her the exact location. I hung up and laid the seat of my car as far back as it would go and went to sleep.

The next thing I knew, I was jolted awake by a cop beating on the roof of my car. They had pinged my phone to pinpoint my location. EMT's showed up and took me to the hospital. They didn't pump my stomach or induce vomiting. They just kept me awake the whole time and kept a close watch on my vitals. My blood pressure was through the roof, so they checked me for heart problems while they had me there.

My best friend called me the next day; I was still in the hospital. She shared with me how she had lost a boyfriend to suicide many years earlier and how devastating that was. Her point really rang true. The longer I stared at those hospital walls, the more I realized I hadn't really wanted to kill myself. Why else would I have sent an email to my loved ones?

I could have just as easily written a note and left it in the passenger's seat to be found with my lifeless body. It was just a seemingly hopeless scenario. I was scared and didn't know what else to do. Instead of reaching out for help and admitting I was scared, I put on a "tough guy" front and internalized my fear. Bad idea! When you do that, it's going to eventually manifest itself, someway, somehow.

After I was released from the hospital, I knew I had to face the music and go to prison. It was the right thing to do because I *had* broken the law. Walking through the front door of a prison knowing you can't walk back through it for six years is a feeling that no poet or scholar could justly describe. And the first time you hear the slam of your cell door behind you is comparable to a cannon going off right behind both ears.

It had been a while since I had read the Bible, but when the ringing in my ears from the slam of the cell door subsided, the first thing that came to mind was the verse Romans 3:23. It talks about how we have all sinned and fallen short of the glory of God. That really hit home. I immediately fell to my knees and began sobbing uncontrollably. The reality of it all became more than I could resist any longer.

It was at that moment that I turned myself completely over to God. I immersed myself in the Bible and was amazed at how much there was to be learned from it. The warden of the prison was more in touch with what was going on in his prison than I thought. After I had been there only a month, he called me to his office and told me how some of his guards had informed him how much I had changed in such a short amount of time.

I was stunned because I hadn't realized it myself. He told me about the prison ministry program they had and asked if I would share my testimony with the other inmates. For those of you who don't know, when a warden "asks" you to do something, it's not really a request. Nonetheless, I was thrilled at the opportunity.

It was all becoming crystal clear now. This is why I was in prison. My testimony of how greed and corruption became a path to repentance and redemption was my reason for being here. I jumped full force into the prison ministry program and spent every waking hour studying the Bible. After three months, I was dealt a major blow. I was informed I was going to be transferred to another prison. This was devastating because I had no idea what kind of ministry program they had, if any at all. The more

I fretted about the upcoming move, the deeper I went into the scripture. At that point and time, Hebrews 11 was my saving grace. It speaks on faith. I had to keep the faith and know that this transfer was for the greater good.

When I got to the new prison, I found out just how true this was. My second day there, I was called in to the warden's office. It was like déjà vu. He told me how the warden at my last prison had called ahead to let him know what kind of positive influence I had on the other prisoners through their ministry program. With that, the warden informed me that he wanted something similar in his prison but didn't have any inmates with the knowledge or passion to pull it off. He asked me if I wanted to spearhead their program.

Was I dreaming?! Needless to say, I went into action. In the blink of an eye, another five months had gone by. I was called in to the warden's office yet again. This time he told me something I was not expecting. He said he was recommending me for early release based on good behavior (due almost entirely to my prison ministry efforts). In a strange way, I was a little sad. The prison ministry had become my main focus and my reason for living. I knew, however, I couldn't pass up this great opportunity to get out early and start my life over again. So, after eight months, I was released to serve the balance of my six year sentence on house arrest and probation.

Before this, did I believe everything happens for a reason? Not really. Afterwards? You bet your ass I do! Without this experience, I would not be the person I am today, emotionally or spiritually. This whole chain of events led to me meeting the woman of my dreams (now my wife). Have I thought about suicide since then? Yes, but I would never, never, never do it because I saw first hand how selfish an act suicide really is. I would never put my loved ones through that kind of pain.

For anyone considering suicide, I would say this to you: Read the Bible, especially the stories about hope and forgiveness (i.e. 1 Peter 1:3-9, 1 Corinthians 13:13, Matthew 18:21-35). Take a really hard look at yourself in the mirror because, no matter how dark the night seems to be, the sun will rise and once again bring light. I love you and pray the best for you all.

4

Firefighter

Let's start at the beginning. The doctor told my mother I would most likely have brain damage in connection with my being born about a month later than expected. As a result, I have been made to feel that I was written off from day one, literally! That led to my excess in mediocrity. Some may say being "average" as a child is great. Try it some time.

My self-esteem problems really began in junior high. I was always pretty hard on myself, but my first "couples" dance gave me the proof I needed to know I was a loser. After much scouring, I found a girl willing to go with me to the dance. That was a major victory in my eyes. The celebration didn't last long, though.

Once we got there, my date quickly found her friends and abandoned me to the bleachers. I spent the rest of the night cowering in the darkness. It was at that point I realized that's where I belonged, where I deserved to be.

That was the first time I ever thought, "I'm better off dead." Contemplating suicide, even for a fraction of a second, is something you can never undo. It's like the old saying, "You can't un-ring a bell." The question is, do you become obsessed with the thought or do you just let it go as a random, ridiculous thought? I became obsessed.

From that point on, I never gave much effort to my schoolwork or to trying to fit in with the "right" crowd. Going back to what the doctor said on the day I was born, I felt like very little was ever expected from me anyway, so why try?! As a B and C student, I never got much praise. But, then again, I never got much scolding either. The middle of the road was where I lived and where I belonged.

The thing that kept me pushing forward was my faith and the officials of my church. The only problem was they weren't really qualified to counsel someone with depression. I was convinced that's what I had. That was a personal diagnosis, of course. I didn't dare go to a doctor because I didn't want to end up in the "nut house." So, I dealt with it the best way I could.

A friend told me about meditation. It seemed a little "woo-woo" for my taste, but I thought "what the heck?" Meditation is kinda like medication in the sense that if you stick with it and do it on a regular basis, it actually works pretty well (it did for me at least). On the other hand, like medication, you start to feel "normal" and decide you don't need to do it as often, or at all. That's when the problems begin to creep in again.

After high school, I began looking for a job. Lord knows I would have never made it through college. I went through the laundry list of typical minimum-wage jobs but never stuck around long enough to get a raise or promoted. Being extremely introverted and totally lacking in self-confidence are not attractive traits to employers. After a lot of soul-searching, I decided I wanted to be a firefighter. I'm not sure if I had a lapse in self-pity or what it was that made me think I could do it, but I went for it.

I found out when the next series of hirings were going to be and I began to get in shape. That turned out to be easier than I thought. Maybe this was gonna work out after all. When the time came, I took the physical exams and ended up finishing near the top of the group. Then they hit me with something I wasn't expecting, a 200 question mental exam. It covered a wide variety of questions that looked at you from all angles. They're fashioned in such a way that you don't really know the motive behind some of them. I was worried the whole time about what they were going to "find out" about me. Luckily, I passed the mental exam, although I was barely considered average (leaning toward not being a good candidate).

They ended up offering me the job and I was head-over-heels excited. For once, I set my mind on achieving a goal that seemed out of my reach, and I did it! It was definitely a rite of passage for me. Something that actually made me proud of myself. After the ecstacy faded, the doubt began to creep in. What was I thinking? Nothing else I ever did worked out. Why would this be any different?

I didn't get invited to hang out with the "cool" firefighters. They'd come in talking about the great night on the town they had or the game they all got together to watch. I felt like I was in junior high again. There were a couple of other guys that I clicked with, but they were "newbies" like me and were in no position to help my career.

Despite the tremendous amount of effort I put into getting physically fit for the job, I began letting myself go. I reverted back to the B and C student mentality and just skated by. That may get you by in school, but it doesn't cut it in a job like a firefighter, where people's lives are in your hands.

After five years of scraping by and a handful of "second chances," I was terminated by the fire department. During my time as a firefighter, I had found and married a nice girl and had a couple of kids. She must have been more impressed by the uniform than she was by me. At least that's what I told myself because why would a woman even care enough to go on a second date with me, much less marry me? That's what the kid in the bleachers inside me always whispered. Well, my termination from the fire department was the final straw for my wife.

We had the typical marital problems like finances and petty bickering, but this was it. She insisted we go to a retreat for married couples with problems. Honestly, it sounded quite ridiculous, but I didn't have the energy to fight about it. Go along to get along. After a couple of days into the retreat, my wife felt like I wasn't trying hard enough (and I probably wasn't) and told me I needed to "get with the program."

At that point I had my own program in mind. I was going to kill myself and be done with all this bullshit. At the next break, I told her I was going to the bathroom and took off walking. I ended up walking two or three miles to where all the vehicles were parked. I found our car and got in. After driving about ten minutes, I found an isolated location and parked.

Once I got there, I had calmed down tremendously. Maybe it was the fact that I lashed out and took control for a few minutes, but I no longer had the urge to kill myself. After I began to really think about what I had done, I got tickled because I had no way to kill myself anyway. I guess I could have driven into a tree or something, but that might not have killed me either.

About thirty minutes after parking, I cranked up the car and headed back to the retreat. My wife was, not surprisingly, furious with me when I got there. She lit into me for five minutes without a second's break. When she finally let me speak, I told her I had left to kill myself. That slowed her down. From then on, she was on egg shells, even after we got home from the retreat. With time, things got better, as did our marriage.

I went to a vocational school to learn how to work on computers. This seemed to be a good fit for me. Once I graduated, I was hired by a call center. Like everything else in my life, the "new" wore off rather quickly. A month into it, I felt trapped and was basically hobbling along.

The pressures of a commercial work environment were way more than I had anticipated. And, again, just like in school, there were "clicks" in the workplace and I didn't seem to fit into any of them. Some of them went to lunch together every day. Others went out for drinks after work most days. Heck, some even slept together!

Despite the misery of it, I hung in there for five years. As a husband and a father, I felt like my family's needs and happiness were much more important than mine. Any suffering I endured was for them. That's how I justified it, at least. That was, until, the day my wife emailed me at work to let me know our bank account was in the "red" yet again. That was the straw that broke this camel's back. I just couldn't take it anymore! To be this miserable and to still get shit from my wife because there wasn't enough money for what she wanted to do. It had to end!

I told my supervisor something had come up and I had to rush home. From work, I went straight to the liquor store. Then I went to the general store and got a bottle of aspirin and some razor blades. From there, I drove to the nearest wooded area that would provide some privacy. My plan was to get hammered drunk so I wouldn't "chicken out" once I started the process. Then I'd take the aspirin to thin out my blood (something I learned during my stint with the fire department). Finally, I would take a razor blade and slice a main artery in my arm.

Once I parked, I started my plan. I used the whiskey to wash down the aspirin (two steps in one!). When the effects of the alcohol began setting in, I got out a razor. It's now or never. Finally, I'll finish something I started! It was at this point that I began hallucinating. There were voices talking to me, but they were telling me not to do it. It seemed like cops or EMTs talking to me, encouraging me, but there was no one around. I yelled at them to leave me alone and to go away.

In a fit of rage, I took the razor and made a long slash up my arm. I smiled and leaned the seat back, knowing it wouldn't be long now. Hopefully, no one would find me for days or even weeks. I wanted wild animals to find my lifeless body and tear me to shreds so there wasn't even a trace of me left. What better way to punish my wife than this? When the kids asked her, "Where's daddy?" she'd have to tell them, "Well, I drove him to suicide . . . and then wild animals ate him."

I scratched out something on a piece of paper that was to be my suicide note. I was so looped out of my mind, there's no telling what I wrote. The note was never found, so I guess I'll never know.

To my surprise, I woke up a couple of hours later. I looked at my arm and there was some blood, but it wasn't from a main artery. It turns out, I was so drunk that I barely broke the surface of my skin and had what amounted to an eight inch long papercut. Since the booze had pretty much worn off by now, I cranked the car and drove myself to the hospital.

Once I arrived, I was taken to the emergency room and treated for my wound. I was in the ER for a total of twelve hours. Since this was a suicide attempt, there were tons of hoops to jump through as far as questions, tests, counsellors, etc. It was quite embarrasing. After they released me from the ER, I was sent to the intensive care unit and placed under observation (suicide watch). During this whole ordeal, my family was in and out, checking on me and reassuring me that things were going to be okay.

By this point, I was actually pretty upbeat. Thinking back to my younger days when I used to meditate a lot, I remembered how much better I felt when I did it in the woods as opposed to inside. Maybe that's what had happened this time.

When I went to the woods, deep down, I knew that's where I needed to be to rid myself of all my negative energy. I didn't need to kill myself, I just needed to go to the woods, slow down, and collect my thoughts. That's when I made the decision to always find time to meditate and reconnect with myself (preferably outdoors).

From this ordeal, I have learned several lessons. Forgiveness is key. I've learned to forgive myself and not be so critical all the time. I have also learned to forgive others. We're only human. Encouragement is another big one. I look back to my childhood and see how if there had been more encouragement in my life, I might have come down from those bleachers and joined in the fun. Gratitude is so important as well. It is like a crowbar. If you can get the tip of gratitude under the rock of depression, keep prying away, because it will let the light of love in!

The time since my suicide attempt hasn't been easy, but it has been much more manageable with proper medication, counseling, and, of course, meditation. I thought mine was an isolated case, but when I started counseling they told me there had been over three hundred suicide cases that came into the same ER as I did in one month.

That is unbelievable! When did the world become such a hopeless place? Now that I am more aware of how my thoughts and actions impact others, I am doing my part, no matter how small, to make a difference. There has to be more compassion and less judgment in this world. Be kind to others because you never know whose life you may end up saving.

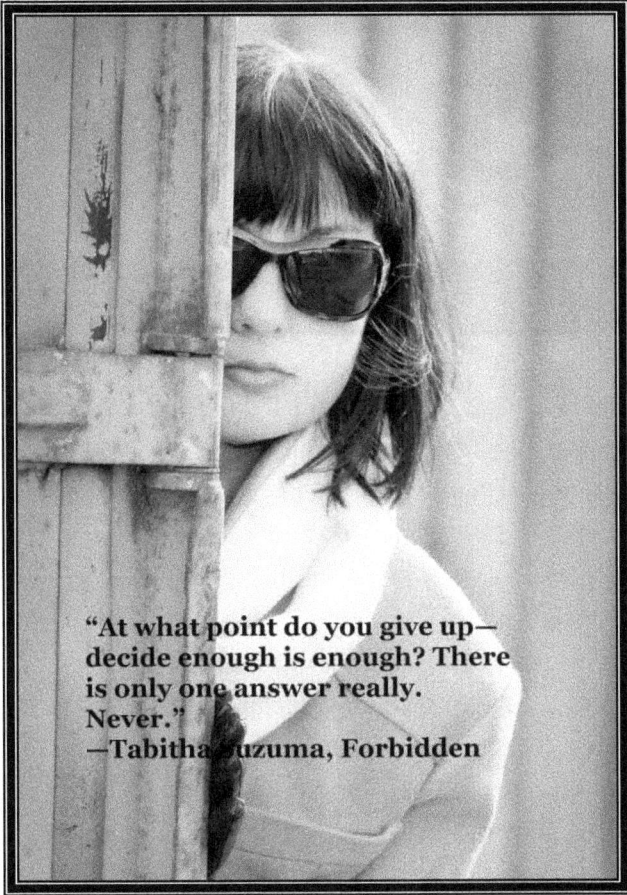

"At what point do you give up—decide enough is enough? There is only one answer really. Never."
—Tabitha Suzuma, Forbidden

istockphoto.com

5

Bewitched

Being a Native American, I believe in the power of natural medicine. To me, it is much more dependable and predictable than "traditional" medicine.

On the flip side, anything that has the power to heal has the power to kill. And it was the latter that I had quite an experience with years ago. I was in my early thirties and the manager of a fast food restaurant.

I took a lot of pride in my job and myself. It meant a lot to me to be respected for my work ethic and dedication. All that changed when I met her. She was eighteen and drop-dead gorgeous. At first, we didn't really get along, mainly because she was immature and wouldn't listen to or follow orders (typical of most teens I knew).

As time went on, she began flirting with me. At first, I ignored it or played it off because I knew it was unethical to date a co-worker, especially since I was her boss. Despite that, I began to go with the flow, so to speak, and we eventually started dating outside the workplace. We kept it a secret because of the ramifications it would have at work.

Well, we didn't hide it as well as we thought. My boss eventually found out and confronted me. I confessed. As a result, they transferred her to a different location. They kept me where I was because they said I was more valuable to them at that particular location. After she was transferred, the relationship became challenging, but we managed.

Soon we began talking about moving in together. Here's the problem. I was already living with another woman! And up until I began dating my co-worker, I truly loved her. Something about my co-worker, however, was so fetching that I was totally engrossed with her. My mind, body, and soul were so totally with my co-worker that I almost felt possessed. This puzzled me because I really was happy with the woman I loved and was living with.

Nonetheless, I decided to leave the woman I "loved" for the girl I "liked." So, I moved in with my co-worker and her mother. I helped pay the bills as my way of contributing to the household. In essence, I became more of a father figure to my girlfriend than a boyfriend in that I was constantly trying to empower her to better herself. She had low self-esteem and I wanted to help her break out of that shell.

In a way, I still saw myself as her "supervisor" like when we worked together. Eventually, this became too much for her to handle because, apparently, it seemed I cared more about helping her than she did. It wasn't until we started living together that I found out she had a problem with pills and alcohol. The longer I lived there, the more she drifted away from me.

After a few weeks, I began noticing she was getting texts on her cell phone late at night (around 2:00 a.m.) on a regular basis. One night, I waited until she went to the bathroom and found proof it was her old boyfriend texting her. When I confronted her, she denied having any feelings for him, but I knew better.

With that, I decided to leave her. No one was going to make a chump out of me! She went on a drinking binge like never before. Even though one of her family members tried to intervene, I was having none of it. I had major trust issues from being burned before and this sure didn't make that any better.

About a week later, she showed up at my workplace saying she was pregnant. Despite my better judgment, I took her back. In the back of my mind, I knew it wasn't going to work. Our lifestyles were just too different. She had too many personal demons and she wouldn't allow anyone to help her.

It only took a week before we had our last face to face meeting and it was pretty hostile. It was at that point we decided to end it for good. Strangely enough, I thought I would feel better, but just the opposite was true.

I basically went crazy. My mind was filled with nonsense and crazy thoughts. The idea of my potential wife and child slipping through my hands was too much. My future was gone! I missed her and wanted to be with her! She was the love of my life! The best times of my life were with her! What had I done?!

Despite my earlier thoughts, I recanted and took her back one more time. By the time I made contact with her, she had already moved on to someone else. That was soul-crushing. I fell into a depression so deep I thought there was no way out. Life didn't make sense. Whenever I went to work, I had to strain to seem happy.

About a month later, I felt an overwhelming sense of sadness come upon me and didn't know why. It was one of those ominous feelings you have when a loved one dies? So, I immediately called my mom just to be sure. She said everyone was okay as far as she knew. I felt better but still prayed about it, mainly for clarity of my feelings.

A couple of weeks later I ran into a friend of mine I hadn't seen in a while. He told me my ex had gotten an abortion. Turns out, it was the same day I had that ominous feeling! The connection to my unborn child had been severed. This made my depression even worse. It was at that point that I *knew* there was no point in living any longer.

On my way home from my shift that night, I stopped at a gas station and used the pay phone (I had lost my cell phone earlier that day). I called my mom to explain to her my situation and to let her know what I was going to do. When she didn't answer, I just took that as confirmation that I was doing the right thing because she wasn't able to try to talk me out of it.

I didn't have any pain medication, but I did have my diabetic pills. So, I took all I had on me (twenty pills) hoping that it would send me into a diabetic coma and I would die. After I took the pills, I went back to the pay phone and called my ex. She didn't answer either, but I left her a pretty nasty voicemail. That felt pretty good.

I got back into the car, leaned my seat back, and awaited death. It was around 2:00 a.m. and I was parked in the edge of the gas station parking lot. With my seat leaned back, it looked like my car was just parked there empty. I had picked the most random location I could so none of my friends I bump into from time to time would see me or know where I was.

I didn't write a note because I figured the act spoke for itself. Before I got too far into it, I pulled my driver's license out of my wallet and held it in my hand so when the cops found me they could easily identify my body. The police regularly patrolled the area I was in looking for "suspicious" behavior. That's why I parked at a gas station. It wouldn't be suspicious at first, but I figured after being parked there for a few hours, one of the gas station attendants might call the cops (at the very least to have my car towed away).

As I started feeling light-headed, I put on a CD of my favorite tribal chanting music and imagined fading away and rejoining my departed loved ones in the spirit world. Much to my surprise, I awoke at 9:00 a.m. I couldn't believe in the seven hours of being parked in the same place in a public location no one had found me or even tried to wake me up.

With that, I cranked the car and went back to my place. It was then that I really understood how much I needed help. And I don't mean a laundry list of anti-depressants kind of help, I mean real, traditional, spiritual help. After researching and calling around, I found a traditional medicine man within a couple of hours of my home. I booked an appointment ASAP.

Early in our relationship, my co-worker had given me a turquoise bear. She said it was a token to help me be strong. At that point, I had no reason to question its meaning or any ulterior motives she may have had. I don't even know what prompted me to do so, but I took it with me to the appointment with the medicine man. Thank goodness I did because all of this was about to make a whole lot of sense.

We had our session. It was very authentic and traditional; just what I had hoped. It definitely put me on the path to feeling better. During the ceremony, I showed him the bear. He immediately saw it for what it really was. All things have the potential to be used for good or for bad. In this case, the bear basically became the Native equivalent of a voodoo doll. The token was given with the negative intentions of me being under her spell. My thoughts and actions all started making complete sense.

Looking back, I didn't even really like her that much until after she gave me the bear. The medicine man said it even made me consider suicide because it was her intention for me to kill myself if our relationship didn't work out. That's the most wicked pre-nup I'd ever heard of.

By the end of it all, I had really learned a lot from my session. The main thing was, don't leave "love" for "like." People can love, hate, envy, or respect you. It is their choice, not yours. You can't (and definitely shouldn't) try to make someone think a certain way about you. Your actions should speak for themselves.

It was a slow, painful process, but after a couple of months, I got better. My ex ended up finding me several years later on social media and apologized for hurting me. Funny thing is, I don't remember her specifically apologizing for putting a spell on me and trying to "curse" me into killing myself! Que sera sera.

My advice to anyone going through a hard time is this: life is what you make of it. Yes, you are going to go through good times and bad, but that's what makes life interesting. It gives you wisdom to help others in need, whether it be a friend or a stranger. There is help out there, professional and spiritual. Miracles happen on a daily basis; I'm living proof of that.

If there's suicidal history in your family (as it was in mine), pay very close attention to your thoughts and actions. Depression can creep up on you like a cat and pounce like a lion. Lastly, it's not worth killing yourself over a girl (or anyone else). It's your life, not theirs. If they don't want you when you're alive, why do you think killing yourself would make them want you (or miss you) any more? Honestly, I have no ill will towards my ex. I appreciate the lessons I learned in the process. Plus, I know karma will take care of her for me.

6

Legally Deaf

The first time I attempted suicide was at age eighteen, but I had considered it several times before that. Having a disability as a child is bad enough, but when you're the only kid in your class with one (or even the classes ahead and behind you), you've got a bullseye the size of a wagon wheel on your back.

When you go to a smaller school, you'd imagine it to be more of a close-knit family atmosphere. In my case, it made me a much easier target. With fewer people to pick on, the most obvious choice was the only handicapped kid in the class.

My problems were apparent from the very beginning. I was born three months premature, weighing a whopping one pound. Initially, I wasn't even supposed to live. The hospital kept me in an incubator for three months before I was allowed to go home. Everything developed properly except my ears and my nasal cavities. As a result, I have about 30 percent hearing in one ear and around 20 percent in the other. Because of this impairment, I don't speak as clearly as other people, or at least that's what I've been told. To me, I sound like everyone else.

The best way I can describe how it feels is this: imagine putting an ear plug in each ear and then carrying on a normal conversation with those around you. You end up yelling just so you can hear yourself through the ear plugs, plus you don't quite pronounce everything just right either.

Well, throughout school, I didn't really have any friends. I was very private and kept my feelings bottled up. Looking back, I realize I was suffering from depression during most of my childhood. At the time, I didn't know what depression was or what it even meant to be depressed. And I certainly was never treated for it. As I got older, school got more and more difficult and the bullying got much more aggressive. The 10th through 12th grades seemed to be the worst of all.

My parents had gotten divorced when I was seven, but my father still came around from time to time, most of the time uninvited. He was an alcoholic and was quite abusive to my mother (even after they divorced). On top of all that, my mom and I lived with my grandmother and it just so happened she suffered from anxiety attacks as well as depression.

That toxic environment was a recipe for disaster. To cope, I began drinking. By age eighteen, I had developed a serious alcohol problem. I guess I didn't learn a damn thing from watching my father. I didn't have enough sense to know that alcoholism is a family trait that I was very susceptible to having.

After graduating high school, I moved away from our little town to the "big city." I thought the change of scenery would be good for me. Plus, I figured strangers would be less likely to harass or make fun of me (at least to my face). I yearned for that anonymous lifestyle that came from being in a metropolitan area. It wasn't long before I met a young man I connected with. We both shared a passion for drinking and partying. Honestly, that's all I was looking for, someone to get drunk with.

After a few weeks of constant binging and partying, my depression got the best of me. Everything began to catch up to me and alcohol couldn't numb the pain anymore. I needed something stronger. My boyfriend and I were having problems and I was just fed up with the world in general. I had been out partying at a club, had gotten drunk on wine, and just flipped out.

After getting home, I stumbled around the apartment looking for a way to end all my suffering. I clamored through the drawers and the cabinets. Then I saw it ... my bottle of Tylenol PM. If a couple of pills usually put me to sleep, what would the whole bottle do? I decided to find out.

I took the whole bottle (with a little more wine for good measure). Stumbling into the bedroom, I couldn't help but laugh because it was going to finally be over, all the suffering, all the teasing, all the pain. I didn't take time to write a note, because, honestly, I didn't think anyone would give a damn. That may be a little selfish on my part, but I wasn't in the mood for caring about what others thought.

When the wine and the pills started taking effect, I began feeling groggy and sleepy and kinda out of it. I lay on the bed with my partying clothes still on. I wanted to be found like that because I wanted to look my prettiest and at peace.

When I was dressed for clubbing is when I felt like I looked my absolute best. Well, as I was fading away, the little dog I'd had for nearly ten years jumped up on the bed beside me. It had the saddest look on its face. I felt it was saying "Mama, what have you done?"

In that instant, I felt like that was God's way of speaking to me, through the only living thing I knew that truly loved me. That was just the jolt I needed to snap back into reality. As a result, I called 911 and told them what I had done.

The EMTs arrived while I was still on the phone with 911. They had kept me on the phone so I wouldn't fall asleep and possibly go into a coma. They pumped my stomach and gave me an IV to reverse the effects of the drugs. That was a first for me. Getting your stomach pumped is quite an awful experience. If you've never had it done, count yourself fortunate. And since this was an attempted suicide, the police had to get involved. It was quite an ordeal, to say the least.

After this, my parents realized just how serious things had gotten for me and finally got involved. They agreed I

65

needed professional help. A shrink. I was eighteen then and I am in my mid-forties now. I've been going to a psychiatrist no less than every three months ever since then (more often when necessary). Throughout the years, I've had the rainbow of anti-depressants, anti-anxiety pills, you name it.

In the early days, I felt like my doctor was nothing more than a pill-pusher. So, I took it upon myself to quit taking my meds (without his knowledge). Mistake! During that three months of "cold turkey," I experienced a plethora of emotions I never knew existed. I now count that among the stupidest of things I've ever done.

Never, never, never quit your meds without first consulting your doctor. Never! While on my "cold turkey" roller coaster, I was commuting to work and had the overwhelming desire to jerk the wheel of my car hard enough to cause me to drive off the bridge into the lake I crossed twice a day.

Folks that didn't know me would just assume it was an accident. Those few who did know me would've suspected foul play on my part. It literally felt like one hand was pulling the steering wheel one way and the other was fighting it as hard as it could. My fingers were gripping the wheel so tightly, they ached for days after that!

I wish I could say that time at eighteen was the only time I ever got to the point of suicide. It wasn't. After that incident, I actually attempted four more times. It was the same modus operandi. Sometimes it was Tylenol PM, other times it was Prozac. But there was always wine. A couple of times, my boyfriend found me and called 911. Once, my neighbor called them because I bumped into him in the hall and told him I was about to do it. Another time, I called them myself. You see a pattern here?

I think deep down I never really wanted to kill myself, otherwise why did I always do it with someone else around or tell someone or call 911 myself? I felt like it was a temporary fix to a permanent problem. There just wasn't any hope in my mind. My goal was to get right to the edge of death and come back, hoping I'd gain some spiritual enlightenment from the process. Alternately, if the EMTs didn't get there in time, it was their fault I died, not mine.

The last time I attempted suicide (about four years ago) was one of the times my boyfriend found me. I was at his apartment. We had been fighting all day and, as a result, I had been drinking all day (maybe vice versa). I'd spent most of the day lounging around in a T-shirt. This time I took a whole bottle of something. I say "something" because I have no clue what it was. I just grabbed a bottle out of the medicine cabinet that felt full and started swallowing. My boyfriend got to missing me and found me in the bedroom.

I was laid out on the floor, naked and sweating profusely. He told me later he had shaken me, but I was completely unresponsive. He actually thought I was dead this time. The EMTs arrived and took me through the same rigmarole I had become accustomed to (stomach pump, IV, etc.). All I remember, however, was a darkness in my mind. I was in a place of total blackness and nothingness. That was the scariest experience of them all because I think I may have actually died that time. The thought of that black void being where I would spend eternity scared the ever-living shit out of me.

That was definitely the last time I attempted suicide. That doesn't mean I haven't considered it again, though. When times get rough, the idea crosses my mind, but I always remember that darkness, that emptiness. I'm afraid if I tried it again, I'd actually succeed. Plus, I think about how it would affect my friends, my family, and even my co-workers. It's a decision that affects everyone around you. That's why I'm sharing my story.

I want others to realize there is hope. You are not alone. Whatever you're going through, it will pass. If you do attempt suicide and are successful, just remember this—there ain't no coming back. That's it. No restart button on this game of life.

I've wanted to tell my story for years but am just now coming to terms with it and am accepting responsibility for my thoughts and my actions. Two years ago, I started going to church and my suicidal thoughts have lessened tremendously. My pastor has been a great counselor and mentor (much more so than my shrink!). I have since been baptized and have a whole new outlook on life.

My goal is to help others by openly discussing my story and sharing my bouts with depression and suicide. It is much more common a thought to have than most people are willing to admit. It is a condition that is treatable, but only if you're willing to open yourself up and reach out for help. There are so many people out there waiting and willing to help, just ask.

7

Boyfriend from Hell

Living in a small Southern town, we were a middle class family with well-educated parents that had high expectations for their four children. I was the only girl and the third of four children. I was expected to do what I was told, do well in school and attend church. My parents were extremely religious and our family life revolved around participating in church activities.

Dad was a deacon and Mother was a Sunday School teacher. I enjoyed church choir, visiting nursing homes to sing for the elderly, Bible drills, and going on summer mission trips. I was rather quiet, shy and never offered my opinions about anything. I tried to please my parents and would have never talked back no matter what the situation. I was known for my ready smile and thoughtfulness. I was considered happy, loved my family and was strongly rooted in spirituality.

Later, I realized that I had not had an original thought until my mid-twenties.

My freshman year of college I was selected for drill team, joined French Club, Baptist Student Union, drama club and the yearbook staff. I quickly made lots of friends and was elected to several leadership positions on campus. I was totally into every opportunity college life offered. I felt that life could not get any better. Football season was exhausting with tons of excitement and travel. The drill team practiced about three hours a day and then there was studying, BSU and a play in which I had a lead and all the other campus activities. My life was a wonderful whirlwind. I dated a little, but mostly enjoyed being with groups of friends.

Just before semester break a friend introduced me to one of the popular guys on the football team. He had all the attributes any girl looks for: handsome, charming and very attentive. By break we had gone on a couple of dates. Early on we seemed to be a great couple. He attended a Christmas program at my home church and briefly met my family. During the break my mom said she liked him, but reminded me that I was young and didn't need to get too serious about one person so early in college. She encouraged me to continue to have fun playing the field and enjoying everything I could. I knew she was right and I totally agreed, assuring her that those were my plans.

During semester break I made excuses not to see him. I had a great time hanging out with hometown friends and being with my brothers. He called a lot and when I'd say I had plans and couldn't see him he seemed so disappointed that it made me feel really bad. One night my three brothers and I were at a church-sponsored function and he surprised me by showing up uninvited. I certainly didn't mind, but my brothers didn't like it at all.

The next morning at breakfast my two older brothers said it was creepy, called him a stalker and said I should get rid of him. I defended him and said he was always welcome at church functions. I guess I assumed they were maybe jealous or questioning my judgment.

The day I was returning to college he called and offered to drive over to my hometown to follow me in his car to make sure I made it back safely. I thanked him for his offer but said no because I wanted to make a few stops and visit a few friends along my journey back. He insisted and I yielded because I knew he had missed me and was just trying to be thoughtful.

I cut out my stops along the way and we drove straight to the dorms. On the road I started looking forward to seeing all my new college friends that would be returning for Spring semester. By the time we arrived I was really anxious to see my roommates and other friends, but he insisted that we spend the evening together having a nice dinner. Knowing he wouldn't accept a simple no, I pretended to have a severe headache and told him that I needed to rest and unpack.

He called my room three times that evening to see how I was feeling. During one of our brief conversations he mentioned that the noise in the room didn't sound like I was resting and taking care of myself. I wanted to believe his actions were out of compassion and genuine concern for me. On the third call one of my suite-mates laughed and called him my shadow, but added that he was a very handsome shadow.

Knowing that I was not ready to get serious with anyone I planned to break up with him. I felt stupid about planning to break up since we weren't officially going together and had never talked about not dating other people. All I knew was that I didn't want a "shadow" or to have to report in to anyone, not at this point in my life. We planned to go out to dinner on Thursday evening and I knew what I had to do. I wanted to have a pleasant dinner and then have a gentle, but serious, conversation about our relationship.

He arrived Thursday evening with flowers in hand. The smile on my face hid my dread as I ran upstairs to put the flowers in my room. Once we arrived at the restaurant, the waiter seated us in a private area and nodded to him, saying he hoped this was what he had in mind. I was relieved myself that we were in a secluded area of the restaurant, but I didn't understand why he apparently had asked for privacy.

The menus arrived but he said we didn't need them because he knew what he wanted us to order already. Glancing at my telling expression, he gently squeezed my hand and said, "I promise I'll never disappoint you." I couldn't believe he ordered for me. That felt like control rather than love. I'm sitting there thinking, Oh Lord why wasn't I just a jerk and break up over the phone or sitting in the lobby of the dorm? I didn't want to hurt him but now I was beginning to get more and more miserable by the minute.

Once our entrées arrived I felt my stomach hurting, heart pounding and flushed with dread. I swear, the absolute second I was opening my mouth to tell him I wanted to end our relationship he reached over and said he didn't want to upset me, but he needed to tell me something. He indicated he'd asked for our secluded seating so we would have complete privacy.

My evening, my future, my life changed in that moment. He prefaced his outpouring by telling me that I was sent by God to be in his life. My strength and my faith had been a great testimony to him. I tried to stop him at that point, but he put his finger to my lips and said, "Please don't interrupt me. You can respond only after you know it all."

Almost crying and gasping to breathe, I insisted that I needed to say something first. Again he touched my lips, only more firmly this time. "No, I said. No. I have to get this out. You have to know. Otherwise it's not fair to you."

The only thing I knew was that it wasn't fair to him to think I wanted to continue seeing him, but he would not let me speak.

Totally defeated, I sat back, somewhat afraid. I tried to focus on his piercing eyes. He shared what a difficult home-life he had. His parents were fighting all the time and they both were considered alcoholics. His mother had been diagnosed with Bipolar Disorder and been hospitalized for treatment several times. His dad was abusive to both her and the children. He said they had never even seen him play football in college. His brother was in jail on drug charges and his sister was single with two kids. He looked at me and said, "You are all I have. Promise me you will pray for us and my family."

I assured him that I always pray for all my friends and their families. I started stuttering trying to move the conversation away from his emotional catharsis, but he totally ignored me and continued talking. He said I was the first girl he could trust in years. He described several girlfriends who had lied and cheated on him. He said they were always flirting with other guys and often putting him in awkward positions of having to defend them when men came on to them.

I could hear my thoughts screaming, "No, no, no, get away"! I knew he was hurting and it was difficult to share everything about his dysfunctional home, but I also knew I couldn't fix his family or fill the emotional void for him. I wasn't in love with him, had planned on breaking up and now I'm feeling so sad for him and actually sad for myself.

At that moment I had no idea what to say or what to do. I suggested that we pray. I held his hand and prayed for God to keep his arms around my friend and bless his life and keep him strong in his faith. After I prayed he opened his eyes and said, "Thanks friend—that wasn't exactly the response I was looking for."

I ignored his comment and tried to choke down my dinner.

In the following days he kept telling me more and more family details. I suggested he see someone in the Counseling Center on campus but he refused. He wanted everything to stay a secret. He wouldn't discuss anything with others on the football team or with our BSU prayer team. I started feeling that the more he shared with me the more dependent and controlling he became.

By February I told a friend that I was almost scared of him. Laughingly, I said, "He's like, I've told you too much and if you leave me I'll have to kill you." She grabbed me and insisted that we tell someone, but I felt that I had to just trust God to get me out of this situation, so I pulled away laughing and denying that I was really afraid of him.

All I thought about was ways to get away from him. Sometimes I actually felt like I hated him. I knew he was in control when I started hating school and not participating in activities I had loved only months earlier. He skipped class to watch me through the classroom windows and he followed me everywhere.

He would quiz me on exactly what I had said to every male I spoke to. He got angry that we had to sit in alphabetical order in biology class and I had assigned seating between two guys. He threatened me if I smiled when we took our French Club pictures for the yearbook because it would make people think I was happy when I wasn't with him.

What he didn't realize was that it was true, I was happy when I wasn't around him. I prayed constantly for God to give me a way out. I would go days not speaking over two words in his presence, but he never noticed my unhappiness and depression. One day he jerked my arm when I started to cross the yard to visit with a guy friend from high school and said, "So you are one of those slutty girlfriends after all."

I wanted to scream out for my friend to help me, to get me away from this monster. Only hours later he asked me to pray for his family, for him and our relationship as if nothing happened earlier. Instead of being even angrier, I felt guilty that I doubted his intentions. I refused to believe he would use prayer and spirituality for evil.

I wanted out and tried to broach the issue often. He always cursed me and called me horrible names, but then quickly resort to tears. Often I would endure his entire tirade but eventually repeat that I thought we needed to go our separate ways. He would apologize and beg me to give him another chance. I just felt like our personalities were not compatible and I was always walking on eggshells and had lost my smile, and myself. I wasn't looking for an apology; I wanted my life back.

He might agree to give me a little space, but every time, within a day or two something would happen in his family and he would become emotional and beg me to stay in the relationship until he got through the crisis.

Somehow I never had enough strength to say no. I felt that as a Christian I had to help him, be there for him and just pray for God to get me out of the situation.

We were a couple by everyone's definition. He was with me or knew where I was every second. My friends and family were polite to him at first but no one really liked him. They all expressed their concerns that I had changed since I met him. They blamed him for my depression and my withdrawal from friends and activities.

Although I knew they were absolutely right, I felt that I had to defend him and be loyal to him if I was dating him. I felt like they judged him too quickly without really knowing his family situation. I believed that God could heal his heart and make him the loving Christian man he could be. I didn't discuss any of my concerns about him with anyone because I knew my brothers would intervene and maybe get someone killed.

By spring we were still together and he had convinced me that I should not try out for drill team for the next year. My family didn't buy my excuse of not wanting to try out because I was too busy. They knew I had loved being on drill team before I met him.

I also dropped yearbook staff because he didn't like me having to work with male staffers. Nothing seemed worth fighting with him over and I capitulated on anything he demanded. Things seemed to continually spiral downward. The more control he exerted the more I gave in. My parents talked to me several times about breaking up with him and getting back to my old self of enjoying college. I tried to hide his behavior from them and only said positive things about him. I asked them to pray for him rather than condemn him. Even with me constantly denying it, they knew he was bad news.

One night we were driving to my parent's house for dinner and I mentioned that I really wanted to be on the drill team and I disagreed that it was morally wrong. I knew Mom would bring it up and I needed to discuss it before we arrived. I was torn between pleasing my parents who wanted me to try out, and pleasing him, who basically had forbid me to try out.

My perfect life of pleasing everyone was quickly crumbling. I was so confused because I knew my parents were right about how much I had changed because of him, but I felt sorry for him and selfish that I wanted to do something that he believed was wrong. I tried to explain my decision to try out, but he got more and more angry, calling me vulgar names and accusing me of being unfaithful to him.

Suddenly, he hit me across my chest and yelled, "It'll be your fault whatever happens. You know I can't let men lust after you while you are dancing and smiling on that damn drill team."

Dinner was tense with my family. It seemed like everyone knew everything, but no one said anything. We all ate mostly in silence with intermittent small talk. As we were leaving, I hugged my parents and said that I had been praying about drill team and felt that God was leading me in a different direction and I had decided not to try out.

They really couldn't argue with me using the prayer card. I walked out feeling depressed, confused, and my only prayer was that I could escape his grip on me.

Later that evening my mom called me once I got back to the dorm. She was crying and said that she and Dad felt they had lost their daughter to a monster. I tried to defend him, but it sounded shallow. She said they had been so proud of me being on drill team and participating in BSU, having a part in a play and now I was doing nothing but what he said to do. She called me his puppet and implied they were disappointed in me. I knew everything she said was right but I also felt that she was trying to boss me around as much as he was.

At that moment I realized that I hated everything and everyone, but mostly myself. All I really wanted was to please everyone. I was afraid of him but I didn't want to be my parents' baby and let them boss me forever. I hated myself for not being able to stand up to anyone, for not having an opinion or being strong. In my effort to be the Christian I wanted to be I had lost my way and was wandering aimlessly among sinners. There was no way out of my situation and I knew it.

For the next two days I lay in the bed telling everyone I had flu symptoms but was too depressed to move. I cried, slept, and cried more. I got up on the third day and walked over to the clinic. I told the doctor that I couldn't sleep and when I did I had nightmares. He prescribed sleeping pills and warned me against taking too many. I politely thanked him and assured him I would use them sparingly.

By that point I had made up my mind and I knew what I had to do. I had no reason to live if I would eventually disappoint everyone who loved me. I walked straight back to my dorm room and took a handful of the pills. I wrote a simple note to everyone who cared about me, saying "Sorry, please forgive me. I never wanted to hurt you."

I didn't die that day but the insecure, person pleaser, without an original thought or opinion did die. I am a different person now. After years of therapy, I began to understand my need to please and how pleasers and controllers end up together. I know nothing about him anymore, but I do hope he got the help he needed. I still pray that he let God help him reach his potential.

8

Big Sister

Being a teenager is tough enough. Being constantly told you're the shortest, the slowest, the fattest, and even the ugliest girl in your class by your peers makes it pretty unbearable. Believe me, my troubles started way before my teenage years.

The farthest back I remember is being three years old, climbing up into the kitchen cabinets, and then cooking my own food. At that time, I was the only child and I was already more responsible than my parents.

My father was a "functioning" alcoholic. By that, I mean he had a job and all that kind of stuff, but he pretty much stayed drunk and was able to maintain the illusion (at least to the outside world) that he was fine. He worked off-shore on an oil rig in the Gulf of Mexico and would typically be gone for thirty days at a time. My mom, on the other hand, was a paranoid-schizophrenic and was gone more than she was at home. For the most part, she was completely non-functional. That left me in charge most of the time.

Once my siblings came along, it didn't take long for me to take on the role as their mother (more out of necessity than anything else). I loved them and didn't want to see them do without. By the time I was eleven, I was driving. It was for anything and everything, from driving my siblings to various functions to driving all of us to school. We went to a rural school, so the other students actually thought it was pretty cool I was "allowed" to drive to school.

Little did they know. I'm guessing the school officials never said anything because they knew my family and knew that was the only way we'd ever be at school. By the time I was thirteen, I was officially in charge of organizing and paying all the family bills. It only took the lights getting turned off three times before my parents agreed to let me handle it.

My family was the definition of dysfunctional. I remember one time when the youngest was only one year old (still in diapers), he got out of the house and was running down the road before we knew it. I got to missing him and asked my mom where he was. Why I even asked, I have no idea . . . She said, "Hell, I don't know. You find him; he's your damn brother!"

Nice, Mom. So I went outside looking for him, calling for him. Finally, I heard a car horn and thought, "Oh shit, he's in the road!" I ran as fast as I could to the road and saw a car had pulled over and the lady in the passenger seat had her door open and was holding him.

When I got there, I could barely breath. I told her thank you so much. She said, "Where is this child's mother?" Without thinking, I said, "I'm his mother."

With good reason, the lady gave me the craziest look. I was only eight years old for God's sake. I thought no more about it until later that evening when the police showed up with a person from social services. It turns out the nice lady from the car had called the police and reported the incident. When they asked to see my mother, I went inside and told her who was there and why. She ran to the door and flung it open. There was a string of profanities that followed that no adult, much less an eight year old girl, should have to hear. It didn't take much of that to convince the police and the social worker to leave.

As time went on, this was what I considered to be a "normal" family atmosphere. Why wouldn't I? I had nothing to compare it to. I was never invited over to slumber parties (or any other kind of parties), so I had no reference point other than what I saw every day. Basically, whatever you get used to is what becomes your "norm."

One night my mother was having one of the worst psychotic episodes I had ever seen. When I saw it coming, I rounded up my brother and my sister and sent them to their rooms. By the time I returned to the living room to check on mother, she had disappeared. Lord only knows where she had gone. I looked around the front yard, then the back. She was nowhere to be found.

After twenty minutes or so of searching, I went back inside. Much to my shock, she was sitting in my dad's recliner with his .357 magnum pistol in her hand with the coldest, most hollow-eyed glare on her face. With the pistol, she motioned for me to come closer.

When I got there she grabbed my right arm and jerked me down in front of her. She slowly pressed the barrel of the gun to my temple and said, "You wanna meet Jesus? He told me he's lonely and wants some company. You ready to die?"

I screamed, "No mama, please!"

She pressed the barrel even harder to my temple and just snickered. She finally let go of my arm and I fell back against the coffee table. She just went back to that cold, dead stare as I ran to my room. I was ten years old.

If all of this going on at home wasn't bad enough, when I'd get to school, I would have to steady myself for the daily barrage of snickers and flat-out insults hurled my way. My clothes were always just at the point of falling apart because they had either been patched numerous times or were actually different useless garments that I had sewn together to make one usable outfit. Again, I thought all the other kids had some sort of dysfunctional things going on at home, probably not a gun to the head, but I figured alcoholic parents at least.

It wasn't until my sophomore year of high school that a girl I had become friends with asked me to spend the night one Friday and I realized just how fucked up my family really was. When we got to her house, I was amazed at how well the yard was manicured, the house was not falling apart, and the wallpaper in each room actually matched on every wall. Her mother welcomed me and took my bookbag. I thought maybe she was checking it for weapons or something. She went over to a line of hooks by the garage door and hung it up next to my friend's. Oh.

When dinnertime came around, they turned off the television and we all sat around the dinner table. Ours was covered with so much crap, you'd need a leaf blower to clean it off. We all sat down. I was about to reach for the food and start serving myself when they all reached their hands out to each other and held hands for the blessing.

My friend held my right hand and her mother held my left. It was actually so nice it made me extremely uncomfortable. Not because of their kindness toward me, but the realization that this was normal, not what I experienced everyday. Holy shit! I was living in a nightmare that no one else in my class could possibly relate to.

What was I going to do? My siblings and I were living in the house from hell. I could not believe that all those years I thought everyone in my class had at least some of the same problems at home that we did. Not even close. This was just overwhelming. The more time I spent with my friend, the more I asked questions about her home life and things her family did. Her mother did all the cooking, the cleaning, and even the laundry. My friend had a couple of "chores" she did. And she actually got paid for doing them! If I didn't do my "chores," the lights would get cut off and everyone would be wearing the same underwear for weeks. And I sure as hell didn't get paid to do any of that! This was too much, too much.

That was it. My days of being the mother to my siblings and the slave to my parents were over. No more! And my classmates could kiss my ass. They wouldn't be able to pick on me anymore either. I was going to kill myself. Maybe that'd make them feel at least half as shitty for picking on me as they actually made me feel on a daily basis.

When I got home, I went straight to my dad's gun cabinet and got his pistol. It was the same .357 magnum my mother had put to my head so many years ago. How fitting. I sat on the end of my bed, just looking at it. How powerful, how pretty, how deadly.

Yes, this would definitely do the trick. I got a pen and paper and wrote a short note to whomever found me. It basically said I was tired of everything; all the cooking, the cleaning, the bullshit. I set the notepad down and turned on the radio. The only reason I can think of for doing that is I love music. It had always played a very important part in my life. Having music in the background when I ended my life just seemed appropriate.

I put the barrel of the pistol in my mouth. I could smell the burnt gun powder from the last time it had been fired. Also, I could taste the gun oil my father had used to clean it. I became somewhat entranced examining the gun with my mouth. I bit down quite hard on the barrel with my teeth. I don't know why I expected it to give at all, but it didn't.

With my thumb, I cocked the hammer back, click, click. Now for the boom. As I rested my thumb on the trigger, I noticed the song on the radio. It was "When the Children Cry" by White Lion. As the song played, I realized I was loosening my grip on the pistol. By the time it got to the guitar solo, my grip had relaxed so much the pistol fell from my hands onto the floor. I heard a scream and realized it was coming from me. All the stress and pain had culminated with this one extreme act of desperation. I screamed and cried for the next thirty minutes non-stop.

Once I had cried until there was nothing left to release, I went to the bathroom and washed my face. Afterwards, I went back into the bedroom and picked up the gun from the floor. I very carefully released the trigger. Before I returned it to my dad's gun cabinet, I grabbed his bottle of gun oil and a rag and wiped over the parts I had touched. That's the mother in me, always cleaning. As I walked out of the room, I noticed the note I had written.

At first, I started to tear it up. But as my hands were gripped to tear the paper, I stopped. Instead, I folded it up neatly and put it in my pocket. Later, I put it in the wallet I carry in my purse. No matter how many wallets or purses I go through, that note is always with me. It is there not only to remind me of how desperate I had gotten, but also to remind me of how strong I was for not pulling that trigger.

Since then, things have not been all peaches and cream. Yes, life at home with an alcoholic father and a psychotic mother was still hard. But it never seemed as hard after that. That event taught me that I am one hell of a tough person. If I could survive that hell-hole, I could weather any storm the world could throw at me. Also, I realized that nothing is worth killing yourself over. If no one likes you, the hell with them. It's their problem not yours.

I have kids now and they are my love and my life. And in reality, I have the best parenting guidelines in the world. Just raise my kids the exact opposite of how my parents raised my siblings and me!

Chin up, my friend. There's always a brighter day coming.

9

Dying For Love

I played football in high school and was decent enough to get a lot of time on the field. Of course that was the criterion for popularity and dating. My grades were pretty good, so even the teachers liked me. I dated every cheerleader and majorette during those four years. Life was easy and good back then.

We got in trouble for stupid things, but nothing really bad. During our senior year a couple of guys got DUIs and that was the biggest news that year. I guess I look back on those days as some of the best days of my life, but I didn't know it at the time.

Over half of our senior class started college, mostly community college, but probably only a fourth ever finished. I flunked out and ended up getting an electronics certificate after working as a bartender and waiter for a while. I got a decent job and life was ok. I lived with two friends and had a company truck, so I felt almost rich.

I spent days working and nights drinking and smoking marijuana with friends. I went through girlfriend after girlfriend, but didn't really want to settle down. They all seemed a lot of fun for the first couple of months and then all the demands started. That's when I usually took a hike. At that time in my life I was not interested in being tied down and being bossed around by anyone. I knew marriage and kids would be around the corner if I got too involved.

All was going well until my company downsized and I was suddenly out of a job, losing income and transportation. It took about six weeks to find another job. During my time off work I became so desperate I ended up selling marijuana to just a few regulars. I tried to convince myself that I needed the money and had no choice, but I knew better.

After starting to work with a much better company I didn't need the money, but continued to deal. For about four years I lived for quitting time to start my nightly ritual of making a couple of sells, then drinking and smoking until I fell asleep.

I don't even know how we got together but I ended up with a girl who liked my habits as much as I did. We didn't have much in common other than our substance abuse. She was high strung, loud and drove me crazy until she would get high then mellow out. Our compatibility was when we were laid out drunk and sucking on a bong.

We went to Las Vegas with friends for a long weekend and I have no idea why, but we got married.

Standing there, both in jeans and T-shirts, we pledged our love for one another. I think we were both too embarrassed to acknowledge how stupid we had been, so neither of us brought it up. It was done.

Married now, we moved a couple of miles away from my parents. They quickly assumed they were welcome to drop by any time. They were none too happy about my sudden marriage or my new bride. We cleaned up our act for a while because we never knew when my Mom and Dad would come over uninvited. My wife often pretended to have plans with her girlfriends if my parents showed up. She wouldn't get home until after midnight, but I really didn't care.

Our marriage was not much to brag about. We fussed and fought all the time about everything and nothing. We cursed and screamed and drank and smoked. Neither of us was happy but didn't do much to improve things. I regret not getting out before she got pregnant but I didn't. I actually stopped smoking and only drank on weekends to try to encourage her to be healthy while she was pregnant. During her whole pregnancy she seemed to hate me. We were so lucky that our sweet baby girl was healthy and not affected by her mother's behavior during pregnancy.

I was pretty happy after our daughter's birth in spite of our bad marriage. I enjoyed taking care of my daughter, but my wife criticized everything I did. Half the time she wouldn't move when the baby cried, but whatever I did to console the baby was wrong.

So why when you have a bad marriage and one baby do you get pregnant again? I'll never know why we let that happen, but we did. Our first daughter was fourteen months old when our second daughter was born. Both girls were beautiful and easy-going.

My wife must have suffered from depression after the second baby. There were times she wouldn't touch either baby for days at a time. She turned to our old habits of drinking and pot to deal with her depression and refused to go to the doctor. We reversed roles and the worse she got the better I got. For the first time in many years I was totally clean.

In the midst of the chaos at home I was recruited by the best electrical contracting company in the region. I was offered a great job with great money. They had random drug screenings, so I had to stay off drugs if I wanted to keep my job. I was making good money and I was glad that my wife didn't need to work so she could be home with the babies. She liked being at home but felt overwhelmed with two babies. She enrolled the girls in daycare and headed for the bar every afternoon.

I don't really know why we got a divorce. We had never been in love nor did we get along, but our girls needed us to be together. Once both girls were in elementary school, she filed for divorce. I begged her to reconsider. I promised to do better, not really knowing what I'd change. I had thought she would go back to work once the girls got in school. In fact, we had developed a pretty expensive lifestyle and we needed her to go back to work. She wanted none of it. She wanted to maintain her lifestyle on alimony and child support.

Once the divorce was final I felt like I had lost everything important to me. I had to argue, fight and demand to see the girls. There were always conflicts in scheduling and my visitation was always what got shortchanged. Angry and depressed, I started drinking again. I couldn't risk smoking because of my job. I felt so rejected. I had been their primary caregiver for years, but now my own daughters seemed to choose their mom over spending time with me.

I criticized their mom when I had the girls, although I knew that was wrong. They would defend her and it would escalate into accusations. I wanted them to know how much I loved them and took care of them when she ignored them. My attempts to discuss the past were ill timed and not welcome. I knew their mother was not who they thought she was. She was deep into prescription drugs, washing them down with vodka. It was my money that paid for everything she and the girls had, yet she tried to turn my girls against me. Years of an on and off relationship with my daughters tore my heart apart.

I got promoted into sales about the same time I met a wonderful woman. We got married and I was happy for the first time in many years. My new wife had a five year old son that I adored. She got along with her ex-husband and they cooperated concerning their son. Maybe I was trying to fill the void of being estranged from my daughters.

I became obsessed with the little boy. I was jealous of his close relationship with his own dad. I knew I was wrong, but I couldn't help myself. I wanted him to heal my broken heart.

When I was around my girls I constantly bragged on my new son. That apparently struck a nerve with them. They seemed hurt by my love for him while at the same time they didn't seem to give me the time of day. My youngest daughter once yelled that she hated me and her life would be better if I was dead.

My wife and I started having disagreements about her son. I gave in to him no matter what he wanted or did. I blocked her efforts to discipline him. I felt the tension and knew that she was discussing my behavior with the boy's father. Finally, I knew I would push my wife away if I didn't stop. That was the beginning of my self-destruction. I failed my daughters and now my wife and stepson.

As a salesman I was no longer required to submit to drug testing. In fact I was expected to take clients out for dinner and play golf, all involving drinks. I picked back up with my old familiar habits as if I'd never stopped. Drinking and smoking helped me forget my failures and pain. I had to travel, so I hit the bars when I was on the road. It got so bad I was starting by mid-afternoon, still on the clock.

When my girls came over I hardly paid attention to them and when my stepson wanted my attention I gave him an excuse. I was in a dark place and drowning in self-pity. I freely gave all the kids money, lots of money. I felt that at least they liked me for my money.

I actually thought I could keep this lifestyle up, but I was wrong. My work suffered and human resources finally called me in and gave me an ultimatum. I was required to submit to an evaluation for substance abuse and abide by the recommendations or be fired. They sent me home on a Monday morning and said to let them know when I had the recommendations in writing.

On my way home I thought about people I knew that had been forced into rehab and then they fire you anyway. I knew it was over. I took my wife to lunch to break the news. Instead of showing any concern, she said that if she had been honest with me earlier and had told me she wanted us to separate because of my alcohol and drug abuse that I might have straightened up sooner.

She was right. My daughters were right. My company was right. I was a failure and they would all be better off if I was dead. I knew if I picked up my gun I could do it, but it would be suicide. My family wouldn't get my life insurance. I needed to have a fatal accident.

When I got home I made the evaluation appointment for Thursday. I knew I would never go, but I was trying to make everything look normal I guess. For the next several days I took care of lots of personal business. I asked my wife for a few days to figure out a plan before I had to move out.

Since she thought I was headed to rehab she agreed. My plan was dramatic. I would tell everyone how sorry I was and that I loved them. Once I was gone they would hold onto my final words convinced I'd had a premonition.

The next couple of days were extremely busy. I visited my parents for a long overdue visit. We talked for hours and as I left I felt closer to them than I had since growing up. I lucked out that my daughters made themselves available for dinner. We laughed and cried and they interrupted my apology to offer their apologies. My wife was reluctant but willing to talk. I didn't blame anyone for my behavior or make excuses. I owned it all and thanked her for the joy she brought to my life. I hugged and played with the little man more than I had in months. I asked if I could read him a story and put him to bed. I had taken care of everything and I was ready to take the final step to make it right. I hoped they'd miss what I could have been, not what I really was.

I figured I'd take the company car. There was no reason to destroy our family car. I knew the curve and exactly where to swerve to the right and go tumbling down into the canyon below. A couple of horrible wrecks there had spurred new reports about the need to extend the guard rail, but it had not been done yet.

I smiled to myself fantasizing that my family may be invited to a ribbon cutting when they fix the deadly curve. They can be proud that my death contributed to something. Actually, I was convinced that I was giving my life for them to have a better life without me around. I had a very good life insurance policy with the company since I had to travel so much.

With tears streaming down my cheeks, I closed the front door and headed to the car. At first I thought about not wearing my seatbelt, but I didn't want anything to hinder a good payoff after the accident. I didn't even use my cell phone while I was driving. I took no chances. As I drove I realized I had not even considered taking a drop of alcohol or drugs since Monday. Well at least they can't blame the accident on impaired driving. I'm sure they will check my blood, but I'll be clean. My family can be proud of that.

The last mile was pleasant as I saw flowers I'd never noticed and the mountains in the distance seemed to beckon me. It was ironic that I had driven this road all my life, but only when I was on my last trip did I appreciate everything around me.

Suddenly, there it was only a few yards ahead.

I couldn't believe my eyes. As a truck drifts into my lane, I scream, "Damn it, get the hell over!" I slam on the brakes and blasted my horn. The kid jerks his head up and tried to swerve, but we hit head-on and end up on the guardrail. The very guardrail I had planned to avoid.

As I lay in the hospital with a broken leg and four broken ribs I had plenty of time to think. My brush with death helped me reevaluate what is important to me. My family rallied around me and supported my decision to go to out-patient rehab after I had recovered from the accident. At that point I had been alcohol and drug free over three months, but I knew I needed treatment to learn how to stay substance free.

The good news is I didn't get fired and my daughters and I are getting along great. My wife and I are in therapy to learn healthy ways to blend our families. We are very much in love. My goal is to never go back to that dark place where I spent far too much time. And now I notice all the flowers and mountains and smile as I thank the kid who saved my life by hitting my car.

10

Hippie

Growing up in the "black list" days of when everyone was terrified their neighbors were Communists and were spying on them, I naturally had paranoid tendencies. My parents taught me the world was a dangerous and fearful place. The bad thing was, I was only six years old! That was very scarring to me as a young child. That would be scarring to an adult, to be told the boogeyman is waiting around every corner to forceably brainwash you to their ideals. For God's sake, where does it end?

On top of all that, my parents fought constantly. Violence and verbal abuse were a daily occurrence in my household growing up. To combat all of this negativity and fear-based thinking, I delved deep into the world of fantasy and make-believe. This was my way of escaping all the potential "threats" that constantly surrounded me.

A few of my closest friends and I would play various role-playing games. We also played whatever sport was in season at the time. Even though I never really cared for sports, I played them so I wouldn't be the odd man out. What I really excelled in, though, were the make-believe games. I loved pretending to be someone else in a world without lines or rules or wars.

That's how it went through most of my childhood. When I graduated high school, I immediately left home. Literally, I moved out the next day. The "hippie" movement was in full swing and I wanted to join in all the fun. Their lifestyle was so in line with my free-spirited, leave this world behind attitude. Drugs were plentiful and I wanted them all. Anything and everything I could do to keep my escape from reality from ending was all I wanted.

During that time, I did odd jobs, mainly to keep me in a full stash of drugs. As a result, I moved around a lot because it was hard to keep a job when you forgot where you worked half the time. They tend to frown on you not showing up for work (especially if it's because you were stoned). After a few years of this itinerant lifestyle, I realized I needed to get some structure in my life. I always heard the military could give you structure. I thought, "Why the hell not?" So, I joined the Air Force.

Now that was a culture shock, to say the least. The first thing they did was cut my hair. They didn't say anything about that in the recruiting office. I was already regretting this decision. Well, it was too late by then. I got through basic training as did everyone else. I have to admit, it felt pretty good to be in shape and be focused for once in my life. Sure, the military teaches you there's an enemy and they're out to get you, but they teach you how to do something about it. All my parents ever taught me was to suspect everybody and to keep my mouth shut. Military life was good for a while. When it came time for me to either re-enlist or leave, I chose to leave. I felt I had learned everything I needed to from them.

After the military, I went back to my wandering lifestyle. At heart, I'm really a student. I love to learn, no matter what the situation or the source. I guess that's why I wandered around so much prior to my time with the military and why it was so easy to return to it. The next few years were a blur, to be honest. I did a lot of odd jobs . . . and a lot of drugs. My military training had been pretty generic. I was good at basic clerical and office work, so that's mostly what I did during my service time. That made it pretty easy for me to get a job on the "outside." Keeping one, however, was a different matter. I didn't forget where I worked this time so much as I just didn't care about going very often. That's why I started moving around again.

Luckily, this was well before the internet days, so it was easy for me to fudge my résumé so they didn't see the longest I tended to keep a job was three months. It took that long for me to get set up, get trained on office procedures, get warnings, and get fired. I had it pretty well figured out. I know, I know, that's no way to live. But when your life revolves around drugs and staying high as much as possible, work is seen as a necessary evil, at best. It's a means to an end. The end being getting (and staying) high.

As luck would have it, I was two months into a job and my boss told me his junior sales representative had quit and was wondering if I'd be interested in giving it a try. My initial reaction was it sounded too much like real work. Then he told me how much money I could be making just by taking over this guy's accounts. I jumped on it. I thought, "no more cheap shit for me. I'll get high on the primo stuff from now on." It wasn't business advancement that motivated me, it was drug advancement.

A couple of months into it, I realized I had already beaten my typical time at a job by a month. I had been so involved with my promotion I had actually been looking forward to work. Wow, who'd thought? Things chugged along like that for a while. Weeks turned into months, months turned into years. Before I knew it, I was living in a tremendous house. I was making well over six figures a year. I was living the dream. Sure, I still got high every once in a while, but it was more to celebrate things like closing a huge sale or to unwind while on vacation.

Things were going so well for me, I began getting quite full of myself. I started thinking all I had to do to get a sale was walk in a corporate boardroom, introduce myself, and hand them the paperwork to sign. Sure, my reputation got me more sales than your typical guy. But when my potential clients began picking up on my conceit and my utter lack of respect for them, that's when things started going downhill.

103

First, it was a missed sale here and there. Then, my big accounts I'd had for years began moving to other firms. When I called them to ask them why, they told me maybe I should have paid as much attention to them *before* they left as I was now, trying to get them back. This wasn't happening! With the loss of clients came the loss of income. All of a sudden, I found myself balancing my checkbook at least once a week. Before, I had gone months without looking at it because I knew there was more than enough money in there. Restaurants that I normally walked up to and got a table without a reservation were suddenly telling me they had "nothing available."

This is when my old habits came back into swing, full-force. I always kept a stash of my favorite stuff at home for "special occassions." That was gone in two days. Now I needed more. The high-dollar dealers I had been going to wouldn't return my calls. I guess word had gotten out I was on the way down.

I know it may sound funny to hear a drug dealer wouldn't want to sell me anything. That's how weird things had gotten. The dealers I had been using only dealt with "upscale" users. It was back to buying from the street corners for me. It was no big deal, though. I just had to find out where the action was.

My fall from grace was swift and unpleasant. I made the most of it. I ended up leaving the firm I was with and switched to a smaller, start-up company. None of the few clients I had left were willing to move their business over.

Looking back, I don't blame them. At the time, though, I was pretty disappointed.

This new firm was tickled to have me because they had no idea how sour my career had turned. In the beginning, it was a little bit of a struggle, as it is with any start-up. Surprisingly, I picked up several clients within the first few months. Things started cranking again. How long would it be before I was able to call my "upscale" dealers again? Yes, that was still a big part of my motivation.

But it was all about to unravel. A huge potential client had scheduled me to come in for my sales pitch. This was going to be my saving grace; the account that put me back on top. When I got there and began setting up in their boardroom, my mouth began watering. It was so beautiful. There were marble floors, crystal chandeliers, and all the furniture was mahogany! This was it. My ticket to the top.

A few minutes into the presentation I was giving the most elegant pitch of my life. Then it happened. I got to the part where I had to really stretch the truth well beyond any sense of believability. This took a level of unscrupulousness that I had always been proud to possess. Something stopped me. Right in mid-sentence. I knew I was about to deceive these people and I just couldn't do it. I turned to the Chairman of the Board and said, "I'm sorry Mr. Chairman, I can't do this anymore."

He said "What, your presentation?"

I said, "No . . . lie . . ."

As you can imagine, the look of shock on his face (as well as everyone else's) was quite apparent. I grabbed my briefcase and walked out, leaving everything else behind. The room was completely silent as I shut the doors behind me.

On the way back to my car, I flip-flopped between laughing hysterically and crying uncontrollably. I can't explain what just happened. Some moral compass inside of me just found its bearings. The drive back to my house was akin to being in the eye of a hurricane. Everything seemed to be quiet and still, with the knowledge that you're surrounded in every direction by impending death and destruction.

I got to the house, went up the stairs to my bedroom, and opened the secret door in my closet. That's where I kept my jewelry, extra cash, and most importantly, my pistol. I grabbed it, looked at it, and said, "Fuck it, let's get this over with."

The moral epiphany I had in the middle of my sales presentation made me realize I was just a bad person. I didn't feel like I deserved to be in the world anymore. If I killed myself, I would be doing the world a favor because there'd be one less asshole for them to contend with. I walked into the bathroom, put the gun to my temple, looked in the mirror, and said, "I can do this if I can't find a better idea."

I just stood there and looked at myself, with the gun to my head. I yelled for help. I'm not sure why, because I lived alone and there was no one there to hear me. I yelled again and again and again, never pulling the trigger. Finally, I looked in the mirror at the gun against my head and screamed, "What the fuck are you doing? Why don't you do it already?"

Truth is, I don't know why I didn't do it. I just set the gun on the counter, walked into the bedroom, and fell face first onto the bed. I stayed that way for the rest of the night.

The next morning, I finally mustered the will to get up and do something about my situation. Without even taking time to change clothes, I went downstairs, got in the car, and drove to my doctor's office. I told him I had a drug problem and needed help. There was no mention of the gun because, more than anything, I was embarrassed. He told me there were several support groups in the local area and gave me some flyers and brochures from the various ones. The one that really caught my attention said something like "Are you restless, irritable, and discontented?" I said, "Hell yes!" to all three.

The brochure had their location and meeting times. There was one that night. That was, without a doubt, the best decision I ever made. Making that first step to admit I had a problem and to reach out for help was the beginning of my road to recovery. Through that group, I discovered spiritualism. That has been my major saving grace. I meditate on a regular basis as a way to stay centered and focused. It also has helped me with any anger issues I've had as well as whenever I'm feeling the urge to get high.

I can truthfully say that one instance is the only time I have ever contemplated suicide. Since I never actually put my finger on the trigger, I'm not sure I was really committed to doing it anyway. I think that was a manifestation of the inner struggle I was having as a result of my moral compass finally kicking in.

However, I feel if I ever do get to that point again, it might be a lot harder for me to stop myself. The reason I think that is I have come to truly believe there is a neurological connection/memory made when you get to the point of seriously considering suicide.

Once you've been to the brink, it's much easier to return. That's why so many people who have previously been to the point of suicide end up actually doing it if they consider it again in the future. The barriers and the taboos are not as strong because you've already worked through them the first time. That's why it's so important to pay attention to those you love for warning signs of suicidal behavior, especially if they've gotten to the edge before and even more so if they've actually tried it.

The "test run" lowers your inhibitions for a subsequent attempt. Vigilance, love, compassion, and forgiveness are so important in combatting suicide. I pray all the best for each and every one of you. Namaste.

11

Lesbian

I'm a lesbian and am proud of it. However, growing up in an ultra-conservative, rural community, that wasn't always the case for me. Homophobia has come a long way in my lifetime. I mean that in a good way, because it has lessened tremendously. Of course, it's still out there. As long as there are two or more types of humans in this ol' world, there is going to be some sort of hatred and/or fear of the "different ones."

The good thing in my case is I was able to keep my fellow students from knowing about my sexual preferences while in junior high and high school. It wasn't until college that I began letting my guard down and exploring my desires. That's the great thing about college. It's a time of experimentation and self-exploration, so you are encouraged to be yourself, no matter what that is. For once in my life, I wasn't made to feel like a "sinner" for being gay. I was actually applauded for my honesty.

It was during my time in college that I began actively dating. The funny thing was, in junior high and high school, most all of my classmates dated fairly regularly, but I never did. So this was all virgin territory to me. Again, where I grew up, homosexuality was extremely frowned upon and heavily discouraged because we were always preached to that "God hates fags."

Funny, I thought God loved *everyone*. Nonetheless, this was all quite new to me and I had to be careful in how I proceeded. There are groups and cliques that tend to form fairly quickly, no matter where you are. College is no different. It didn't take me long to find the gay-friendly crowd. Once I started hanging out with them and getting to know the local hangouts friendly to us, I became a lot more socially active.

I started hitting the dance clubs (not that I'm a dancer, I just love the environment). Well, that's where I met her. My goddess. I knew from the moment I saw her that I'd found my true love. She was everything that I had ever dreamt of in a woman. I had to play it cool, so I waited for her to exit the dance floor. When she got to the bar and placed an order, I motioned to the bartender and said "it's on me."

That got my foot in the door. With that, we began talking and, what do you know, we had so many things in common. From our struggles in a small town, to our newness to the whole dating scene, it seemed like we were separated at birth. We even loved the same music! It only took a couple of dates before she was as convinced as me that we were meant to be together, forever. And so it went.

We moved in together the next semester of college. And we lived together throughout the rest of our time there. Neither one of us had much direction. We just studied the basic curriculum and coasted through school. My life was being fulfilled by her companionship. School was just something to do to pass the time. After we graduated, we moved out of state to a more progressive-minded city. It was still in a conservative state, but the bigger cities like the one we moved to tend to be a lot more open-minded to the whole gay scene.

Once there, we both began looking for jobs. Again, we hadn't really majored in anything, so neither one of us really had any specialized skills. She liked movies, so she applied for a job at the nearest movie theater. Turns out they needed someone to work the box office. Perfect! Now we could see movies for free any time we wanted.

Now, what did I like to do? Well, I love to cook and I love to eat. So, I started looking for jobs in the food service industry. Turns out, any decent paying job in the food industry requires experience. Oh, well, might as well start at the bottom and work my way up. That's the American way, right? I looked around and applied at a few places needing dishwashers (with a chance for advancement). Advancement? Was there any chance for demotion? There's only one way to go from washing dishes—up. Finally, I got called in and got a job washing dishes. Basically, they said "if you show up tonight, you've got the job." So much for a résumé and three references.

After a couple of weeks on the job, my supervisor asked "Why the hell are you washing dishes?" I said "because it's my job." Her point was lost on me. She said I was way too smart and hard-working to be scrubbing dishes the rest of my life. With that, she put me on the line as an understudy of her head chef.

Yes, working the line was a long way from being head chef, but it was a start. I didn't realize how much I hated washing dishes until I didn't have to do it anymore. Things progressed and I moved up and up over the next six months. What I didn't realize was things at home weren't going so well. I was so engrossed in my job and my newfound career-path, that I had been neglecting the true love of my life.

At first, she was dropping subtle hints that we needed to spend more time together. Eventually, it was outright demands for my time. Looking back, it was so obvious. But at the time I just couldn't see it.

After a while, the longer I spent at work, the less she seemed to care. It almost seemed she began being less excited to see me come home than she was to see me leave, unlike my sweet little dog. He was *always* glad to see me come home, no matter what time of the day or night. I was so focused on moving up the ladder in our kitchen, I didn't waste more than two seconds worrying myself with what she thought anymore.

It didn't take long for that "cold water in the face" moment to finally come about. As I was getting ready for work one morning, she said we needed to talk. Nothing good ever follows that statement. I told her I didn't have much time because I was already running late. She said it wouldn't take long. And it didn't. She basically said I had to choose between her and my job. What? She sprang that on me as I was walking out the door.

I told her it was my job that was paying most of the rent and the bills, unless the electric company was willing to take vouchers for free movies. That didn't go over too well. I told her we could talk more about it when I got home. She said, "No thanks."

I said "whatever" and slammed the door on my way out.

Here's where it gets even better. I drove the regular forty-five minutes to work, through the snow. After getting there and starting my daily routine, it was less than half an hour before I was called into the front office. That was quite odd because that rarely happened. The few times it had was because I was getting promoted. Maybe this day was going to be all right after all.

Wrong—I was fired.

They said it was because I didn't get the salad station prepped the night before. That made no sense because my cooks were stretched so thin they couldn't do anything but get that night's service taken care of. We were staffed to handle five hundred covers a day and my staff was made to do five hundred covers a shift.

This was just great. Now I had to drive forty-five minutes back home (through the snow) and deal with the crap waiting for me there. Now that whole argument about how I was the major bread-winner of the household was really going to come back to bite me in the ass.

When I got home, I found my girlfriend in bed with another woman. My mind went numb. It took me a minute to realize this was something that had been going on for a while because my initial thought was, "How the hell did she find another girlfriend so goddamn fast?"

That's when I realized she had been seeing someone behind my back. The job I loved so much and dedicated so much of my time to really paid off, let me tell you. It cost me the love of my life. And for all that hard work and dedication, I got fired for not stocking the salad bar one time. I was in such shock, I just grabbed a bag, threw some clothes in it, and left. I went over to a friend's apartment and stayed with her for the time-being. I hated to leave my dog behind, but pets weren't allowed at my friend's place.

In the meantime, life went on as usual. I had an appointment for an endoscopic procedure that I really needed to get done. Luckily, I still had the remainder of the month on my health insurance, so I went ahead and had it done. The friend I was staying with took me to my appointment. It was nice of her to be so helpful in my time of need. Or so I thought.

When I woke up from the anesthesia, I looked around for her, hoping to see a friendly face. Maybe she had stepped out. Once I got my bearings and checked my personal items, I noticed all the money in my purse was gone. The person whom I thought was my only friend left had just robbed me. That was the final straw.

I decided to go home. My parents' home. My real home. I went over to my (now) ex's house, got my dog, and cleaned out the rest of my stuff. She already had her new girlfriend moved in with her. That didn't take long. It helped me realize I was making the right decision.

On the way to my parents' home, all I could think about was running my car into a tree. I didn't think I could take any more stress. I had finally reached my breaking point. I started scanning the landscape along the roadside. Which tree would it be? There weren't very many big trees close to the road. How big would it actually need to be?

Then I saw it. Off in the distance, about a mile ahead, I saw a beautifully majestic oak tree. It had to be nearly a hundred years old. Oh, yes, that would work perfectly. I started picking up speed, partly because I wanted to hit it as hard as possible, but mainly because my heart was racing with exhilaration at the thought of dying.

Just then, my dog woke up, looked at me with the sweetest face, and gave me a really good doggie kiss. It was at that moment I thought, "I can't hurt this sweet, innocent, little dog. He didn't do anything wrong."

So I eased off the accelerator and got back down to the speed limit. Then I looked in the rearview mirror, told myself to grow up, put on my big girl panties, and get a grip. I could get through this because I knew there were so many people back home who loved me and would support me through anything. They always had before.

When I finally got home and settled in, I talked to my parents about my next steps. They never knew about my suicidal thoughts because I was in such a good mood by the time I got there. They helped me put together a résumé (yes, I finally needed one) and I applied for several jobs. Shortly thereafter, I got a call for a temporary job that ended up being so much better than my last job. Later, while still working the temp job, I got called in for an interview for a chef position at another restaurant I had applied at before even taking the temp job . . . and got it.

Everything worked out for me, eventually. The lesson I have taken away from all of this is when things get bad, there's almost always something greater just around the corner. You just have to be willing to receive those blessings when they make themselves available.

Never give up.

12

Overweight Child

The idea of fat people being born with a great sense of humor is purely a myth. It is developed over many, many years as a shield against the pain of constant ridicule and rejection. Sure, I can make people laugh at the drop of a hat, but it's mainly as a distraction from my size and the underlying shame I've been made to feel.

My weight problem began rearing it's ugly head around the second grade. It didn't take long for my classmates to take notice and to take aim. Sure, the jokes hurled by second graders aren't the most creative or whimsical, but they do sting nonetheless.

This petty teasing continued for a couple of years. That's when it got much worse. In between the third and fourth grades, I grew exponentially. And now my weight problem was not only receiving continuous mockery from my classmates, it had attracted the attention of kids in other classes.

In a perfect world, I'd run home to my parents and they'd say things like, "Oh, no, honey, you're beautiful on the inside" or "People don't pick on folks unless they like you."

Yeah, right. When I'd come home complaining of the harsh words and cruelness of my schoolmates, my dad would offer his share of insults to the laundry list. The loving advice I got from him was, "Lose some damn weight and maybe they'd quit picking on you!"

Instead of being able to offer up any comforting words, my mom was focused on trying to at least shut my dad up so he didn't hurt me any worse. That led to knock-down, drag-out fights with shoving, screaming, and the occasional physical exchanges. That created more guilt on my part because somehow my being overweight not only drew unwanted insults from my schoolmates, now it was causing my parents to fight.

If I wasn't fat, I figured, none of this would be happening! It was at this point in my life that I really began questioning life. Yes, as a fourth grader. I felt so alone; like there was no one who cared about me—the fat me, at least. No person should ever be made to feel that way, especially a child. This was my life for several years.

Fast forward to the seventh grade. After yet another one of the countless days of mockery, I was sitting on my bed at my wit's end. Something just came over me and I decided to kill myself. Why the hell not, right? There was no planning, no strategy, just a wish for death. My mind was racing. How would I do it? What would I use? How long would it take?

My parents were downstairs, so I couldn't explore the house for various options. I knew my mom's sleeping pills were in her bathroom cabinet, but I couldn't get to them without her seeing me. My dad's guns were in his closet, but they were out of the question as well. So, I looked around the room to see what I could find as my instrument of death. I looked and looked and looked and then—there it was, my bath robe. It had a nice, strong belt on it.

I took the belt out of it's loops and went into the closet. As I sat down, I closed the door. There was no hesitation. I tied the belt around my neck, gradually making it tighter and tighter. I felt my eyes bulging and could hear my heartbeat in my ears like a heavy metal drummer pounding away. Honestly, I thought I would feel panic or fear, but it was quite peaceful. Now my troubles would be over. The laughter would stop.

As I was drifting away, I heard someone calling my name. An angel . . . my spirit guide . . . God? No, it was my mother calling me to dinner. You know when you're abruptly awakened by a terribly annoying alarm clock? That's exactly what I felt at that moment.

My mom's voice snapped me out of my journey to the other side before I could finish the job. I don't exactly know why I stopped. Maybe it's a primal instinct to respond to your mother's voice, just like feeling the impulse to answer a ringing phone or shake a stranger's outstretched hand. Whatever the reason, I loosened the belt from around my neck and exited the closet.

I looked in the mirror and could see some serious marks on my neck from the belt. If I went downstairs like that, I know it would lead to a firestorm of questions from both parents (leading to my dad's insults, my mom's defense, and yet another round of fights).

So, I hastily looked around the room for a way to conceal the marks. Luckily, I have a love for elaborate neck chokers. I put one on and headed downstairs. For the next several days, I didn't leave my bedroom without one on.

I wish I could say that was the only time I ever considered suicide to the point of acting upon it, but it's not. For several years after the first attempt, I have to admit, things did get a little better, comparatively speaking, of course. My peers still picked on me, my dad still verbally abused me, and my parents still fought. However, my attempt at suicide did open my eyes a little. For a while, my perspective on life was a little brighter.

Strangely enough, one of the reasons was because I had actually proven to myself I had the nerve to try to kill myself. I know that sounds strange, but, for someone who had been told her whole life she was fat, worthless, and would never amount to anything, I felt a sense of pride that I had had the "guts" to try.

Of course, there were semi-serious episodes of rebellion on my part. Like a pressure cooker, I had to let off a little steam now and then to keep from exploding.

After all, I didn't want to have to wear chokers the rest of my life. My dad was famous for his verbal abuse, but even more menacing than that was how he controlled mom and me with money.

Don't get me wrong, we were a long way from being rich. What little discretionary income we had was dangled over our heads like a golden carrot. He had no trouble spending most of it on booze and other nonsense, but if we wanted something it turned into a big production of how hard he worked to get his "stinking paycheck." At one point during my eighth grade year, I decided I'd teach my father a lesson.

One night, after he had passed out, I mean, fallen asleep, I took all the money out of his wallet and the keys to his van. I swung by my friend's house and asked if she wanted to run away with me. She said, "Sure, why the hell not?" We hit the road like teenage versions of "Thelma and Louise." After two days of binging on junk food and sleeping in my dad's van, we returned home. Neither of our parents had called the cops or reported us missing.

At the time it seemed like a blessing. It wasn't until years later that I began to really think about that. Did they really care so little that they didn't want us to be found immediately? Or maybe they were just embarrassed to think about others in the neighborhood finding out how shitty a bunch of folks they really were by causing their kids to run away.

The next year, in the ninth grade, my mom transferred me from the school I had attended my whole life to an alternative school for troubled kids. I don't think she really discussed it with my father, she just did it. She didn't explain to me at the time why I was being transferred (and we have never discussed it since). I believe the episode with the van made her finally realize that I had more than "teenage" problems and could see that time wasn't healing old wounds.

Lord knows my home life wasn't helping any either! I have to admit, this was a tremendous turning point for me. Little did I know there were other kids out there just as screwed up as me, some even worse! For once in my life, I felt "average." I know most people strive for greatness, but when you live in an emotional gutter, average looks pretty darned good.

The alternative schooling was so good that it helped me survive the balance of my school career with only whispers of suicidal thoughts. Several years after school, sometime in my mid-twenties, the suicidal demon reared it's ugly head again. Even though I had learned to live with it, my weight was greater than it had ever been before. Again, I had come to grips with it, but apparently my family had not. Talk about beating a dead horse, a dead, bloated one! By now, I had a job and was living on my own. I went to my parents' house for a courtesy visit. For whatever reason, I felt like I was in the seventh grade all over again.

Old habits die hard, I guess. One thing led to another, words were said (screamed is more like it), and blows were thrown. Yes, really. This time it was more of my mom than my dad. I couldn't believe it. Good for you, mom.

With several choice expletives, I ran out the door, got in my car, and sped home. My breathing was to the point of hyperventilating. My heart was beating so hard, I could see the veins in my neck in the mirror . . . thump, thump, thump! Why, why, why? What the hell! Why is this happening all over again?

When I got home, I threw my keys in the general direction of my kitchen table, kicked over a couple of chairs, and screamed at the top of my lungs. Then I got that feeling again. Fuck this, fuck them, fuck it all!

I ran to the bathroom and scrambled through the cabinets and drawers. Ah, there it was—my straight razor. I slid down the wall onto the floor and just stared at it and giggled. This time, there's no one around to stop me. I'm going to cut my wrists from my hands all the way up to my elbow, the "right" way.

I started cutting my hands and legs. Then they began to look like patterns. How cool! I began spelling out words like "pain," "death," and "hell" on my extremities. The act of carving on myself and the coinciding pain were almost orgasmic. By the time I realized it, three hours had passed. It seemed like mere minutes. Strangely enough, I felt so good after mutilating myself, I had forgotten all about suicide. I stumbled into the bedroom and slept for twelve hours. What a release that all had been.

The next day I awoke to blood-stained sheets and caked up pools of blood on my bathroom floor. It's amazing how much blood you can lose and still live. By this time the pain from all the cutting had really set in. My extremities were throbbing something fierce. It hurt like hell when the water from the shower head hit my body. After my shower, I took inventory of the damage I had done to myself. It was going to be much harder to cover all that up. Luckily, it was cooler weather so I could wear long sleeved shirts and long pants without raising any eyebrows. The marks on my hands were a little harder to deal with. After experimenting with makeup, I was able to find a combination to match my skin tone and that did the trick.

That was the last time I considered suicide to the point of nearly acting upon it. After that episode, I reached out for professional help. It turns out I'm manic depressive with mild schizophrenic tendancies. I basically cope with my mental condition and my emotions day-to-day. I see a shrink on a monthly basis and take my meds every day. I'm married now and my husband has been a great support for me. He knows a little about my past, but definitely not the suicide stories. I just don't think he's ready for that yet. He keeps a close watch over me and knows the warning signs for when I'm going into either my manic or my depressive state.

We have kids now as well. They're a little big for their age and I am so terribly afraid that they will have trouble being picked on. I want to be the strong, supportive parent that I did not have. At least I'll be able to recognize the symptoms if they do get bullied. Even greater than that, though, is my fear of either one of them inheriting my mental condition (even a sliver of it). I'm hoping that I've suffered enough for all of us and it'll end with me.

I wanted to share my story with you because I want to help others, whether you're the one suffering the torment or it's someone you love. If you're the one actually doing the bullying, pay close attention. This story is especially for you. I want you to see what happens to someone who's seen as an outcast, a loner, or a loser. They have feelings and the words you jokingly fling at them hurt so much worse than you could ever imagine. The sting may only last a day or two, but the scars, well, they last a lifetime.

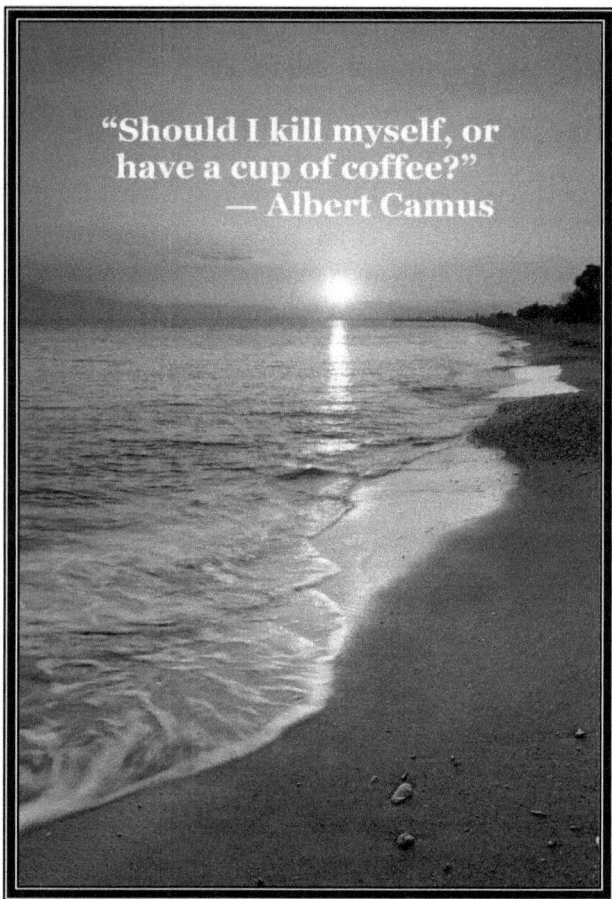

"Should I kill myself, or have a cup of coffee?"
— Albert Camus

istockphoto.com

126

13

Star Student

Sitting on the edge of my bed with my teeth clinched tightly on the barrel of a .44 magnum, my life was seconds away from ending. A hollow point bullet was chosen so there'd be little room for error. The idea for using a .44 magnum came from all the times I heard Dirty Harry say how it could blow your head clean off.

That was perfect, because I wanted my brains to be all over the wall behind me. And man, oh man, whoever found me was going to get a taste of the horror that constantly wracked my brain. My bedroom was the perfect location because that was my fortress of solitude, the place where I always returned when things got rough. It was like the womb I could re-enter at will.

Nothing made sense anymore. No one cared (or so I thought). Then it happened . . . A voice popped in my head saying "not yet." That was the moment I snapped back into reality and realized just how serious things had

127

gotten. Suicide would be just another way for me to avoid responsibility. It's funny, I had shot that pistol so many times before, but never, never had that trigger felt so big. It's as if it was twice as wide and nearly impossible to pull, thankfully. Sure, I had toyed with the idea of suicide several times, but never had it gotten this far along.

It started years before with a life of "potential." If you've never been singled out as "the one," count yourself blessed because the word "potential" is so heavy. The burden it places on you can be devastating. You ace a few exams and all of a sudden you're the benchmark of success for the whole class.

From now on, when the teacher calls on you in class, you had better know the answer. Otherwise, everyone will start thinking you're a slouch. After so long, it seemed people were looking at me and saying "he had so much potential." As if my window of opportunity had passed.

I made straight A's in school and was an above-average athlete, but there was always someone better, someone smarter, someone stronger. It was simple enough to keep up appearances so everyone was "fooled." But with night came the demons.

Solitude was my best friend and my worst enemy. Coming from a family of rough and tough farmers, I felt keeping it to myself was my way of staying strong. Weakness comes in many forms, however. Much to my ignorance, I thought admitting to it was the biggest one of all!

Competition at home was stringent to say the least. Grades, sports, our parents' and our siblings' affection. Constantly battling was a daily occurrence. Rarely did a day go by that someone wasn't jockeying for first place in whatever the flavor of the day was. You win some, you lose some. It was first place or no place, of course. And if you don't cheat, you don't care. That's a mantra I was introduced to at quite an early age. Maybe not the most healthy approach, but, guess what, it got results by God.

As time went on, I learned about our family history of bipolar disorder, dementia, and alcoholism. Isn't that a toxic combination? There's nothing like roasting marshmallows over a fire doused in gasoline, kerosine, and napalm. At that point, my thoughts began to shift from "what's wrong with me" to "now I know what's wrong with me." It sure would have been nice to know that prior to the bedside bonanza I had planned for myself. Oh well, there's some comfort in knowing, I suppose, but it didn't make things any easier.

The bad thing was, I now had something to blame for my failure to maximize my "potential." Instead of doing like a convict who'd discovered his own personal jailhouse Jesus and using that as a building block for my strengthening, I used it as a crutch. Anytime I couldn't accomplish a goal or felt "down in the dumps," I just blamed the family curse. It stung a little at first, but over time, it began to feel like a warm bath that was always waiting for me. At times, all I felt I was good for was converting oxygen to carbon dioxide and I figured I'd probably screw that up from time to time.

At the time in my life when most of my friends were dating and partying, I focused even harder on schoolwork because I wanted to be seen as the "smart one." The teenage years were no time for fun. It was a time to be building your resume so you could get into a good, no, a great college. Admittedly, my dad's influence was reflected in that mentality; however, I took it to the extreme. What good was it to be an average (or even above-average) student when you could be the best? Isn't that what life's all about, work hard so everyone will be impressed. Then they'd know you were living up to your potential. The hours and hours of sacrifice spent studying would be worth it, right?

When I say I studied, let me tell you, that's no joke. I'd get home and do whatever chores needed to be done, eat supper, and get after it! I would study in my room until my parents went to bed (their bedroom was right beside mine) and told me to do the same. I'd pretend to go to sleep. When I could hear that they'd fallen asleep, I'd cut on my little nightlight and start back studying. When I'd start getting sleepy, I would hold the book up over my face so if I dozed off, the book would drop on my face and wake me back up.

I went at least a decade without going to sleep before midnight. After a while it became a badge of honor I gladly wore. Come morning, I was back at it. While using the bathroom, I would take my notes in with me and read them. Finally, the bus ride to school in the morning would be used as my final "review" time for any tests that may be forthcoming that day (even potential pop quizzes). I wouldn't say I was obsessed, just disciplined.

When it came to fun, I saw what my friends were doing as a major waste of time. It seemed ridiculous because I thought, years from now, who's gonna remember what they did on their nights and weekends? Little did I realize at the time, that's the whole point. The old adage that youth is wasted on the young was an understatement in my case. But, at the time, it all seemed worth it because years from now you can always look back at my school transcript and see how "smart" I was. That was results-driven and tangible, unlike "fun." Build that résumé, baby!

Fast-forward to the edge of my bed, sitting there with my "Dirty Harry" pistol and a hollow-point .44 bullet ready to "show them." Whatever or whoever that was that said "not yet" saved my life. Whether you call it divine intervention or just a rude awakening, it was at that moment that my life changed. The studying, the tests, the grades, they all seem so fucking ridiculous. Isn't that the point? Sure, all that stuff's important to a degree, but not to the point I had taken it. It was how I defined myself, and more importantly, that's how I wanted everyone else to define me as well. But I realized that if I pulled that trigger, everyone would realize just how big a phoney and a fake I had been all those years. That thought helped bring it all home.

131

I knew my parents, my siblings, and my friends would have all been terribly distraught. Sure, everyone knew I worked hard in school and dedicated myself to my studies, but no one knew how deep the obsession had become. The adrenaline rush of getting singled out by the teacher as the only student who scored perfect on a test was my main addiction.

It's dangerous when you're the addict and the pusher. All I needed to do to get a fix was to be the best, the brightest, and the smartest. My most favorite thing of all was being the "curve buster." On tests that were significantly harder than normal, a teacher would proclaim ahead of time that they would adjust the scores for everyone based on a curve.

That meant, if the highest score was sixty, they would add enough to that one to bring it up to an "A." At my school, that was a ninety. When I knew there was going to be a "curved" exam, I would study doubly-hard to make sure I scored the highest. So many times after grading, the teacher would announce, "Well, normally I would adjust your scores based on a curve, but we had one student who made an 'A' on this test."

I would start grinning, waiting on them to call out my name. Inevitably, my name would be called and the rest of the students would give me the meanest stares they could conjour up. Boy, if looks could kill. Under my breath, I always muttered, "You should have fucking studied harder, slackers."

Needless to say, up until that point in my life, I had lived a very selfish, a very sheltered, and a very narcissistic life. I saw the world from only one perspective—mine. The consequences and repercussions of my thoughts and actions to other people were irrelevant. Winning was the most important thing. Remember, if you don't cheat, you don't care. My "potential" had almost killed me, literally.

From that day forward, I broadened my perspective and gradually began restructuring my values to include others. For the longest time, I never told anyone about this, not my friends, not my family, no one. Even now, the only person who's ever heard the entire story is my spouse. One of the main reasons I kept this quiet was because the thought of going to a psychiatrist was definitely out of the question. I didn't want to share my deepest, darkest secrets with a shrink, only to get sent to the "looney bin" or put on "crazy" pills.

I'll admit, a lot of that had to do with foolish pride, too. Having said that, I'm more than twice the age now that I was then (and much, much wiser). It's funny that time has given me much more wisdom than any book ever could. Back then, I would have argued you under the table on that point! Wisdom is acquired, not learned. And what I wouldn't give to go back, sit down on the bed beside that troubled teenager, and say the following:

"It's okay to be scared. It's okay to be second best. It's not worth killing yourself over. I promise you! With much sincerity I can safely say that I can barely remember one instance of being singled out in class by the teacher as the only person who aced a test. I know it seems important now, but in the long run, it's not. Seek help. Confide in someone, anyone! You won't be locked away or put on a fistful of dope. What you're feeling is not unique. Please know that things do get better. Focus on being happy, not victorius. I love you."

Since that fateful day on the side of my bed, things have, indeed, gotten better. Whenever I didn't do well on a test (or as well as I would have liked), the earth didn't stop spinning, the other students didn't point at me and laugh, and I didn't think about killing myself anymore. Well, let me rephrase that. I didn't think about killing myself to the point of revisiting the bullet sandwich I almost ate. Whenever I'd get a little down and out, I would be sure to remind myself, "not yet." Has it been easy? Of course not. Has it been worth it? It sure beats the alternative.

14

Teenage Mother

It was many, many years ago when I was young and stupid. Of course, you couldn't have told me that at the time. True love conquers all, right?

It started when I was sixteen years old and the "it" boy at school starting paying more and more attention to me. At first, I thought he was just being friendly, then I realized he was actually attracted to me.

What made me so special that the most popular boy in school wanted to go out with me? I was never encouraged or praised much at home, so this type of attention was overwhelming (and very much appreciated).

It all started with innocent flirting in the shared class we had. Spanish, I think it was. He was a senior and I was a junior. The more the school year went along, the more intense (and less innocent) the flirtation got. As you can imagine, this led to other things.

You have to remember, this was a different time and "good girls" didn't go parking with boys. Well, I was tired of being a "good girl." I wanted to keep the most popular boy in school happy or I was afraid he'd find someone who would.

Needless to say, parking led to me losing my virginity and my innocence. Because no one ever told me about sex, I didn't know anything about protecting myself from pregnancy. You guessed it, my first time led to my getting pregnant. I was in a world of trouble. I began my senior year as a pregnant, unwed mother-to-be. This was a nightmare. It got to the point that I couldn't stay awake very long in any of my classes. As a result, I ended up dropping out of school.

I will give my boyfriend credit, after it got to the point that I couldn't hide it any more, he proposed to me and we got married. It was a "shotgun" wedding for sure. I told him we didn't have to get married because he had so much potential and such a great life ahead of him (without me). He said no, it was his responsibility, too. His friends, on the other hand, made my life a living hell.

Living in a small town where everyone knows everyone's business, the townspeople feel like it's their job to protect the good name of one of their finest. And that's how they saw my husband. He was the "golden boy" of the community. That's why they came to hate me so much. They saw me as the Jezebel who seduced him and ruined any chances of a fairytale life that they, the townspeople, had dreamed up for him.

It didn't stop there. Normally, your family is your rock, your foundation you can count on. Not in this case. My parents brought up every chance they could at how I had not only ruined my life, but I had ruined my husband's, and would soon ruin the life of my (unborn) son. My mother was relentless. She screamed at me whenever I was in earshot. With no support structure, I felt totally and utterly alone.

My husband was in his first year of college and worked constantly (whenever he wasn't in class) to make ends meet for us. Initially, after we were married, I was still living with my parents. But with no end in sight of their undying love (of torturing me), I ended up moving in with my husband at college. That made things a little more bearable, at least from the support standpoint. My husband was great to encourage me, the few times we actually saw each other. Mainly, the lack of constant nagging from my parents was a welcome relief.

When my son was born, I was seventeen. I looked so young (more like thirteen than seventeen) that most people thought my son was my little brother. Let me tell you, that was quite embarrassing. At first, I tried to explain to folks that he was my son. But I realized by the looks I got that people thought I was some sort of inbred, poor white trash that got knocked up at thirteen.

Meanwhile, my husband couldn't keep up the pace of working, going to school, and being a father. The only logical decision was for him to quit school. Of course, the choir of judgmental assholes began chiming in again about how I had ruined his life by "getting" pregnant. It's funny how it seemed to all be my fault for allowing myself to "get" pregnant! No one ever chastised my husband for playing a part in the process. That's just what guys do, right? They sleep with girls, but if one ends up pregnant, it's always the girl's fault.

After he dropped out of school, we moved back home to our small town. Things at first weren't too bad. There were adjustments, but I chalked that up to growing pains and the move. The more time went on, I began to realize that my husband no longer laughed, he no longer had fun or enjoyed anything. This really weighed on me because the man I fell in love with was a funny, happy-go-lucky guy that was the life of the party everywhere he went. That man was gone. Maybe everyone was right. Maybe I did ruin his life.

The more time I spent at home alone raising our child, the more I pondered that very thought. Soon, I quit thinking "maybe" and began thinking I did ruin his life. What kind of person was I? How could I take a person so beloved by his friends, his family, and the whole damn town and reduce him to a minimum-wage earner, a teenage father, and a college dropout?

To a seventeen year old mother in a small town, with no friends and no support structure (even from my family), this became unbearable. I had no social life, no intellectual stimulation, whatsoever. I had become an outcast with my family and the entire community.

When I went to the market, I tried to time it so I ran into the least amount of people possible. Even if no one spoke to me, I could feel their judgmental eyes upon me. Depression really set in at this point. Even though I loved my husband and my baby so very much, I just felt like a total failure. I didn't have any idea what I was doing as a wife or a mother. There was no real role model in my life. And I sure as hell couldn't cook, other than warming up soup.

My life seemed like such a waste. I had such high hopes for myself before all of this. My passion was (and still is) art. Also, I loved writing. It seemed now that any plans of become an artist or a writer were long gone. Honestly, I never wanted kids. I never wanted to get married either.

Out of sheer boredom one day, I decided I'd try drinking. I rooted around the cabinets and found a bottle of vodka. I'd seen plenty of people drink it, so I figured, what the hell? I turned up the bottle and ended up spitting it halfway across the room. Bad idea! That stuff tasted nasty to me.

Later in the day, I made a call and bought a "matchbox" of marijuana. This was a first as well. The whole process was so foreign to me that I didn't realize until I had the weed in hand that I didn't even know how to roll a joint. So, I ended up giving it away. Finally, I found a bottle of muscle relaxers and took all of them. I'm not sure how, but my day had gone from boredom to curiousity to suicide.

This was about three in the afternoon and my husband normally didn't get home until six. So, by the time he got home, I was passed out on the bed. When he got home, he didn't even try to find or check on me. He just went straight to the couch and plopped down in front of the television. Later that evening, my mother called to check on me (to holler at me was more like it). My husband rarely answered the phone, so when it rang about ten times, it actually woke me up enough to pick up the phone.

When I did, I could hear it was my mother, but I couldn't speak. The best I recall, I made some grunting noises or something to that effect and hung up. Not long after that, my mother showed up and took me to the emergency room. They pumped my stomach and the whole nine yards. The most embarrassing thing of it all was, the doctor in the emergency room was someone I knew very well. After they sobered me up, I had to explain to them what happened and what I had taken.

That was the beginning of a new journey for myself. It was the wakeup call I needed. Not long after the suicide attempt, my son and I moved out on our own. It was the most difficult and the most refreshing decision I had ever made in my life.

There were the naysayers, of course. But aren't there always? Back in those days, unwed mothers carried one hell of a label, especially in a small, conservative town such as mine. By this point, I had really quit caring what people thought of me. That was a great step forward for me at this point in my life. The liberation of the first time truly feeling self-control and self-reliance is indescribable.

My life since then has not been easy, by any means. However, I learned so much from that whole experience. It taught me how fragile life really is. In an effort to end my temporary suffering, I attemped to commit a permanent act. Because I was in a place of such hopelessness and despair, I thought there weren't any options. I thought I had not only ruined my life, but I had ruined the life of my husband and our innocent child.

If everyone kept saying it, it had to be true, right? It had gotten to the point that I thought my life was laid out for me and my dreams were gone forever, that I had to give up my ambitions of being an artist or a writer because I had gotten pregnant. That could not have been further from the truth. How can your life be totally and utterly defined for you at seventeen years old? That's the most ridiculous thing I've come to realize. My life had barely begun and I was being told it was basically over.

With several decades of wisdom gathered between then and now, I would love to go back and sit down with that terrified and hopeless young girl. I'd let her know that no matter what everyone tells you, love begins within. If you love yourself, it doesn't matter what everyone else says. It's irrelevant. It was not solely your fault for "getting pregnant," the guy had something to do with it, too. Sex is a shared responsibility between two people. It's not a game or an amusement park ride. The child was the result of two people's actions, not yours alone.

It's okay to pursue your dreams. It's okay to have your own life and your own career. Women are strong by nature and you are so much stronger than you give yourself credit for. Don't let the world dictate what kind of life you're going to have because "that's just how it is." Most people are too afraid to venture outside the box. Trust me, as an adult, you are going to live there, my dear.

15

Poor Little Rich Kid

When did I first think about killing myself? That's easy—seventh grade. I was living with my mom and her husband (my stepdad, not my real dad). My mom was a nurse and my stepfather was a very successful surgeon. Having said that, I'm sure you're thinking, "Wow, she must have lived the charmed life if her stepdad was raking in the dough."

Sure, publicly we had to portray the "cookie cutter" family with a picket fence and all that. But behind closed doors it was much different.

My parents did a lot of "blue blood" partying. By that, I mean they hit all the elite social functions where everyone got together to kiss each others' asses and get stoned. They weren't alcoholics because only poor people could be alcoholics.Yeah, that's what they kept telling themselves.

Well, those parties were definitely no place for a kid. As a result, I spent a lot of time alone. Being that age and alone so often was a dangerous combination, especially with all the pills and booze they kept in the house. It started with experimenting. I'd go through their pills and take one to see what happened. If I felt ambitious, I would pour myself a "sophisticated" drink. I made sure I held my pinky out when I drank. I had to be as classy as my folks, right?

After several adventurous experiments, I became rather bored. Little did I know all these "harmless" pills were taking a toll on my body and my mind. My appetite had become rather sporatic and my mood swings were quite dramatic. My parents, however, didn't seem to notice (or care) because, to them, it was just the typical behavior of a teenage girl. Plus, they weren't there enough to even notice a pattern in my behavior.

The total lack of attention I was getting, along with the extreme mood swings, really began to wear on me. One night when my folks were off at yet another party, I became completely fed up. I decided I wouldn't just experiment with a mixture of pills, I'd take enough to kill myself. By now, I considered myself an expert on the rainbow of pills my parents kept in their medicine cabinet. I didn't know them by name, but I knew them by color.

I knew which ones sped me up and which ones turned me into a zombie. This was no job for the speed pills. Before I was done selecting, I had a double-handful altogether. This was going to be one hell of a ride, straight to zombieland!

I went to the dining room table and made a nice little pile of my colorful selection. Before taking them, I decided I needed something good and potent to wash them all down. I went to the liquor cabinet and grabbed my stepdad's favorite bottle of Scotch. I knew it was his favorite because he bragged to everyone that ever came over about how much he spent on it.

Here I was, sitting at the dining room table with my neatly arranged concoction of death. It's now or never, I thought. One by one, I began taking the pills. It seemed like it was taking forever, so I began taking two, then three at a time. Each time, I was chasing it down with that "wonderful" Scotch. It didn't taste so wonderful to me. It tasted more like shoe polish.

By the time I got to the end of the stack, I must have taken around fifty pills. They were already taking effect because I was getting cross-eyed. When I looked at the bottle, I realized I had drunk nearly half the bottle, one sip at a time! Even though I was doing all of this to kill myself, the only thing going through my mind at this point was, "Holy shit, my stepfather is going to go into orbit over me drinking his Scotch!"

I grabbed the bottle and started feverishly looking around the kitchen for something to pour into the bottle to make it look fuller. Then I remembered we had some iced tea in the fridge. Yeah, it's the same color as Scotch. He'd never know the difference. Plus it tastes a hell of a lot better than that shoe polish crap anyway. That's how it is when someone has more money than sense. They buy things just because they're expensive. Clothes, vehicles, jewelry, Scotch.

I began pouring, spilling more on the floor than what actually made it into the bottle. Nonetheless, I got it pretty much full and placed it back in the liquor cabinet. That was close.

By this time, I was stumbling and knocking over stuff, left and right. I figured it wouldn't be long now, so I headed toward my bedroom. I don't remember actually getting there, but somehow I did. The last memories going through my mind as I was fading into darkness were about how wonderful it would be to be dead. No longer would I have to listen to my stepdad brag about how important his job was and how many people were still alive because of him.

Guess what? I'm dead because of you, you stuck up, pretentious, self-righteous asshole! That would be my final gesture to him. I hope he choked on it. The thought of a suicide note was tempting, but I thought it was better for them to spend the rest of their life wondering what exactly it was that ultimately led to my suicide. The more they struggled with an answer, the more they'd blame themselves. Or, at least, that's what I was hoping.

When my parents got home (at their normal, ungodly hour), they peaked in to check on me. I know this because the sound of them stumbling through the house normally woke me. This was quite a surprise to me because I was supposed to be dead by now. Why wasn't I dead?

I immediately fell back to sleep. Much to my surprise, I woke up at my normal time the next morning. Sure, I was hellaciously tired, but I was alive. What had I done wrong? Surely I took enough pills to kill an elephant, or so I had thought. Plus, I had one heck of a hangover from that Scotch. This was turning out to be one hell of a day already.

So now, I began getting scared because I didn't want my parents to know what I had done. If they found out, they may send me to one of those hospitals for crazy, troubled teens. I'd seen enough after-school specials on television to know I sure didn't want to end up there. I kept telling myself, "Act cool, act cool, act cool."

When one of them would ask me a question, I felt like it was all happening in slow motion. I'm not sure if that's because I was freaking out or if it was just a side effect of all the stuff I had taken the night before. Each answer I gave them was methodically weighed out before it was given. In my effort to seem normal I was acting anything but normal.

As the morning passed, my mom suggested she and I go out for brunch. That was something that we did from time to time that I actually enjoyed. It would've been very suspicious of me to turn that down. So I went. I thought, by now, I was pretty much in the clear.

For whatever reason, when we got to the restaurant, some of the drugs I had taken began kicking back in. All of a sudden I felt extremely tired. It got so bad that I began dozing off in mid-sentence while talking to my mother. It was at this point my mother began questioning me, trying to figure out what was wrong. Initially, it was concern that I was having some kind of medical emergency. The longer it went on, she began to recognize the signs of over-medication. She knew because she had taken enough pills in her life to know the symptoms first-hand.

She called for the bill and we cut our brunch short. By the time we left the restaurant, I was beginning to feel fine again. That's when the hard questions began flowing. Mom drilled me on what I did the night before, what I had taken, how much, etc. Initially, I denied doing anything wrong, but she wouldn't budge.

Finally, I confessed to taking "a few" pills out of boredom. Remembering those after-school specials, the word suicide never crossed my lips. I told her it was my first time to do anything like that and I was sorry.

She made me swear on my life that I'd never do anything like that again. However ironic, I did just that. And, to be honest, I meant it. With that, my mother told me she would not tell my stepdad what I had done. She said he would not be as forgiving and would send me to a boarding school if he ever found out.

I wouldn't give that pompous bastard the satisfaction of having a reason to get rid of me. As lonely as my life had become, I could not have imagined it without being able to see my mom on a daily basis. That's just what I needed to get my mind right.

Now, to present-day. I'm thirty-nine years old with children of my own. Have I considered suicide since that lonely night in the seventh grade? Sure I have, but not to the point of actually gathering up pills to do it. Being a mother myself, I can see the incalculable amount of pain it would cause me if one of my children killed themself. Knowing that, I am so glad I never put my own mother through something like that. It would have been absolutely inhuman.

The main lesson I learned from all of this is suicide is never the answer. You have to think about everyone except yourself in that case. The people who love you, love you no matter what. You may not think so, but they do. Killing yourself to get back at your loved ones is the most careless and selfish thing a human being could ever do.

I promise you, things will get better. It may not be today, tomorrow, or even next month, but it will get better. Think about this: would you let the seventh-grade version of yourself pick out your clothes or the hairstyle you would wear for the rest of your life? Not hardly, right? Now, with that in mind, would you let them decide the fate of your entire existence? As an adult, I know I wouldn't, but, yet, I almost did.

16

Saddened Husband

For two months, those pill bottles taunted me every time I opened the cabinet. I had a prescription for Lorazepam that I only used "as necessary." Well, lately it had become very necessary. I wondered if 1-2 pills took the edge off, what would two whole bottles do? Each bottle held sixty pills and they were both pretty much full. Would that be enough to end my pain, or just enough to prolong it for another couple of days?

I was itching to try it but was afraid it wouldn't be enough to finish me off. The thought of using a gun had crossed my mind, but that was way too messy and would certainly not look like an accident. I doubt two empty Lorazepam bottles would look like an accident either, but it would at least make for a nicer viewing at the funeral home.

You may be asking yourself, how could it have gotten so bad? Let me tell you all about it. No marriage is perfect, no matter what the window dressing may portray.

I have to admit, though, that ours was much better than average, or so I thought. Throughout our ten years together, we had our share of ups and downs, but nothing out of the ordinary. Like most couples, finances were a hot topic from time to time.

I will admit that when it comes to finances and our family budget, I can be quite the stickler for details. When we would have a windfall of money from various projects I would prepare a budget to show how, where, and when the money was to be used (extra payment on the mortgage, pay off a minor loan or a car loan, etc.). If it was enough, we would sit down and plan out a nice exciting (and relaxing) vacation.

My wife did not have a lot of parental support in her earlier years. When she wanted to join a club or venture into extracurricular school activities, the answer was almost always no. The main reason was her parents didn't have time to shuttle her around to various places and events. If it was strictly financial, that is one thing, but the fact that they wouldn't take the time to support her was the most damaging, at least in my opinion. That's why I tried to always make a point to support her in any and every venture possible.

It didn't matter to me if any of her requests seemed bizarre or far-fetched, as long as she was happy. I wanted to make up for those "lost years" of childhood exploration that I was fortunate enough to have. There were so many things over the past ten years that I can barely remember.

The point is, if she wanted to do it and we could afford it, she was going to do it.

I know how important it was to me that my parents supported me in all of my hair-brained ventures growing up. I felt like this was my chance to "give back" by providing her the benefit of childish indulgences that she so drastically craved (and needed).

Little did I know that I was laying the groundwork for a lifestyle that we would not be able to support. Over the years, the missed opportunities of childhood morphed into adulthood wants. I'm talking about the kind of trips and vacations you work your whole life for and plan to do "someday." Don't get me wrong, I enjoyed the trips and self-pampering vacations. But again, it was setting a precedent that was becoming harder and harder to maintain.

When I lost my job of nearly a decade, we had to really tighten down on our spending, or at least, that was the plan. There was a pretty good severance check from my job and I had a good bit of money squirreled away for a rainy day. Well, that rainy day turned into rainy months.

Losing your job in one of the worst economies in the past few decades is not something I would recommend. No matter how much experience you have and how much of an education you have, if companies aren't hiring, you're out of luck. And applying for jobs beneath your qualifications and your experience only put you in the "overqualified" pile. You can't win for losing.

To make our money last longer, I revisited our budget and adjusted it in the best manner I could. I sat down with my significant other and explained it to her the best way I knew how. Her lack of attention or enthusiasm for the changes concerned me a little, but I thought it was just because it was a little overwhelming, not to mention, quite unexpected (considering my job was with such a secure, family-oriented company).

I knew it would take her a little while to get accustomed to the toned-down spending, but after a couple of months of reminding her about the budget changes, all I ever got was "Well, we need what we need." That's when I realized I had created a monster. There are essentials in life that one needs and then there are wants. When wants and desires are seen as necessities, the money starts evaporating.

I thought maybe I hadn't explained myself or the situation well enough, so every once in a while I would sit her down and go over it all again. After a couple of these "budget sessions" things began turning sour. It got to the point that whenever I mentioned the word "budget" she would get extremely defensive or quite flippant.

I began changing up my strategy and tried various approaches . . . good cop, bad cop, indifferent cop. None of them seemed to work. Her response to my repeated pleas for reigning in the discresionary spending was, "it's your fault for spoiling me!" That's gratitude for you...

I know some of you reading this may be thinking, "Why didn't he just smack some sense into her?" Well,

I'm just not that kind of guy. Her last husband had abused her (mentally, physically, and emotionally). I had determined very early on to never treat her with such disrespect as the last guy had. Never once did I lay a hand of anger on her, never drank alcohol or did drugs, never sold drugs, and never cheated on her, all things her last husband did. Like I said earlier, I was determined to be everything she deserved in a husband.

Well, this is when the overwhelming sense of depression really started to take hold of me. My family has a history of depression, bipolar disorder, and dementia. Even though I had only shown slight symptoms of depression in my past, that didn't take away the underlying threat of its existence. My symptoms were so obvious (in hindsight).

I began sleeping a lot longer on a regular basis. My weight began to escalate because I fed my sadness with my drug of choice, food. The term comfort food is an understatement in my case. I put so much thought into every meal because the combination of foods and spices had to be just so. It was my way of focusing on something I could control and I could enjoy.

Even though we shared the same house, our lives began slowly but surely drifting apart. She became engrossed in her virtual life on social networking sites and I focused on food. It's so bizarre when two people who've know each other for so long become almost strangers, even though they share the same bed.

Days turned into weeks, weeks turned into months. Looking back, it's almost a blur. As the money withered away, I tried harder and harder to find a job. But by that time, it was the "holiday season." From my experience in the corporate world, I know that once you begin to approach Thanksgiving, most companies hit "auto-pilot" and cruise through the rest of the year. With that being the case, very few even entertain the idea of hiring anyone.

"Let's wait til the first of the year to worry about that."

Things began getting darker and darker in my mind. My weight kept going up and I honestly could have cared less. My wife was all but an avatar at this point. It definitely began seeming hopeless. The thought of suicide had skated across my mind over the years, but it was never really a serious consideration. But now . . .

I'm such an analytical person and I just couldn't make the calculations in my head work out. I didn't see any way that things were going to work out. For several years, I've had a term life insurance policy on myself for $1 million. There's one on my wife as well. The thought of harming my wife never crossed my mind. However, I began giving a lot of thought to harming myself.

Back to the pill bottles in the cabinet. How many were enough? If I took over 100 pills, would it kill me or just relax me so much that I'd pass out and shit all over the bed?! Would it put me in a coma for a few days? If that happened and I got sent to hospital, how would we pay for it?

155

We didn't have any type of health insurance because I was unemployed. On top of that, I'd have the shame of being a failure at suicide! To me, suicide itself was not shameful because, in my mind, I was doing it to relieve my wife of the burden of a fat, worthless husband. On top of that, she'd get $1 million tax-free and could spend money to her heart's desire. She could go back to living the accelerated lifestyle that I had originally set up for her. All's well that end's well, right?

Needless to say, I fought those desires to take the pills. I did reach out for them on a couple of occasions, but quickly put them back. I'd shake out a couple of pills "as necessary" and let them do their work. Up to that point, my wife never knew I was suicidal, I suppose. For that to happen, I would have had to post it on a social networking site for her to have seen it anyway.

Finally, I broke down and confided in her that I was in a terrible place in my life. That it was most likely the lowest point and the deepest depression I had ever felt. I begged her to help me get out of this funk. I told her I needed her now more than ever and to please help me. For the rest of my life, I will never forget her response. With an icy glare, she said, "There's nothing I can do for you. You're on your own."

I was absolutley crushed. All the years of me catering to her every wish and desire, no matter how ridiculous, summed up in two of the most heart-wrenching sentences I'd ever heard leave her lips.

I was dumbfounded and absolutely clueless as to what had just happened or why. Somehow I pulled myself together and struggled to keep going, alone.

What's the most ironic thing about all of this? A fews days after my desperate plea for help to my wife, she informed me she was moving out. She had been planning it (virtually and realistically) for a while. Her reason was she couldn't be around my "negative energy" and had to think about herself. Plus, she said she wasn't sure if she loved me any more anyway.

Turns out, she had another guy already lined up to "tend to her garden" so to speak. Now I was really glad I had not killed myself. That would have played so perfectly into her plans, it would have been kismet. She could have been the grieving widow, excuse me, the rich grieving widow. Her boyfriend would've really loved me, too. He could've stepped into one hell of a scenario (the caring shoulder for the grieving widow, excuse me, the rich grieving widow to cry on, all without the "homewrecker" stamp to contend with). And my family would not have had the slightest idea that she was planning on leaving me, or the fact that she already had a boyfriend in the shadows.

What have I learned from all this? I've learned that things are not as bad as you think they are in your own mind. While I was blaming myself for our problems and our situation, I later came to understand that marriage is definitely a partnership that takes work from both parties. It is for better or worse, both the good times and the bad.

No one person can be "perfect enough" or "tough enough" for the both of them. No matter how bad you want success and happiness for someone, it is inevitably up to them whether or not they embrace it. The "virtual" world is just that, virtual. When you exit that "reality" there is still the world of flesh and blood to contend with.

Embrace life, embrace love, embrace happiness.

"No. Don't give up hope just yet. It's the last thing to go. When you have lost hope, you have lost everything. And when you think all is lost, when all is dire and bleak, there is always hope."—Pittacus Lore, *I Am Number One*

istockphoto.com

17

Sexually Abused Child
Part I

There are two parts to my story because there were two times in my life where I got to the point that I felt like suicide was my only option. This story is about the time I was twelve years old. When you think of a twelve year old girl, I'm sure the last image that comes to mind is a little girl planning how to end her life. Well, I wasn't your typical twelve year old.

Looking back, it's much easier for me to see the root of my issues. At a very early age, I was sexually abused by someone close to me, a family member, actually. It happened during the single-digit years of my life. As an adult, there are so many things that I wonder about—what made him pick me, was I that sexually desirable, was there anything I could've done to make him not want to touch me? Realistically, I know those questions are irrelevant because sexual predators and child molestors have no morals or scrupples. All they care about is satisfying their most basic, carnal urges no matter how they get it or whom they have to hurt in the process.

Going back to me at twelve, I would consider myself to have been an ackward child, but not terribly different than any other young girl that age. I wasn't popular by any stretch of the imagination either. However, I did have a couple of girls I would hang out with from time to time.

The school I went to was your typical public school. It wasn't a mega-school and it wasn't extremely rural either. All-in-all, I'd say I was a typical kid in a typical school. The main difference between me and my classmates was that I had been repeatedly sexually abused in the years prior.

Even though I had a couple of friends, I felt alone most of the time, like I didn't really fit in anywhere. As an adult, that's not really a big deal, but to a twelve year old, that is the entire world! The amount of heartache and sadness I felt at that age would be overwhelming for me even as an adult. Some people like to say, "If I could go back to those days with what I know now . . . " Well, not me! There's no amount of money that could make me relive that horrific time in my life.

The darkness and depression I was experiencing was only compounded by my lack of overall social interaction. At least I had what I considered to be my best friend to lean upon. That's where I was gravely mistaken. I found out the hard way that it was more of a one-sided friendship. One day on the playground, I approached my friend and asked her if we were still going to see a movie that night. To my surprise, she glared at me and said, "My plans have changed. And just so you know, we're not friends and I never really liked you anyway. Leave me alone!" I was completely taken aback. I stood there speechless. She and some of her "real friends" walked away. That was the final straw.

I had felt anger, sadness, and depression for some time now, but this episode of humiliation and betrayal was more than I could handle. I told my other friend what had happened and that I was having thoughts of harming myself. That was just too much for my friend's twelve year old mind to handle. She just said I was being silly and blew it off. The rest of the day at school, all that was on my mind was the thought of killing myself. I felt that if life was this fickle and I could be so easily betrayed and discarded, what use was there for going on any longer.

After I got home from school, I began putting my plan into action. I had laid out the details in my mind thoughout the day and had finalized them. What I had decided upon was something clean and easy. I didn't want it to be messy or a spectacle. With that in mind, I decided that taking some sort of pills would be the best option. At twelve, I knew next to nothing about pills or medicine in general. That was my mom's job. I always took whatever she told me to when I was sick. Well, I knew I was sick now, just not in a physical sense.

The evening played out like any other typical school night at home with the family. We watched a little television, ate supper, and watched a little more television. The main difference this time was I had the thought of suicide on my mind the entire time. I took some level of pleasure in knowing that my family had no idea what was going through my mind. In reality, that was just another reason for me to do it, because my family never knew what I was thinking.

At one point during the later television session, I slipped away from the family over to the cabinet in the kitchen where my mother always got stuff for me when I was sick. As I said, I knew nothing about medicine other than you take it when you're sick. I looked through the cabinet and found two bottles. One was Tylenol and the other was Dimetap. I knew Dimetap had something to do with allergies; I couldn't remember what Tylenol was for. I took out two of the foil packs from the Dimetap box and took five or six of the Tylenol pills. On the back of one of them it said something about not taking it with alcohol.

Not a bad idea! So, I went over to the adult cabinet under the kitchen sink and looked through it until I found a bottle of what I knew to be alcohol. Looking back, they probably all were. But at that age, I had to keep looking until I found one I recognized from the television commercials. With the bottle in hand, I got all the pills together and took a few at a time, each with a swig of alcohol. The funny thing was, I don't even remember tasting the alcohol at all.

I put the alcohol back in its place in the cabinet and went back into the living room with the family. It wasn't

163

long before bedtime. Normally, I wait until the morning to take my shower for school, but this time I took it before going to bed. My reasoning was, since I was going to be dead when the morning came, I wanted to be clean when they found me. Again, I didn't want anything messy. That included my appearance. Some time during the night, around 4:00 a.m. I think, I woke up and went to the bathroom. At that point, I didn't feel groggy or even sick. After going to the bathroom, I climbed back in bed.

At 6:30 a.m. the alarm went off to get up for school. By now, I knew my attempt had not worked so I just wanted to continue with my normal routine and pretend like nothing ever happened.

When I got to the kitchen for breakfast, I still felt fine. However, when I ate a banana, I immediately threw it back up. It was at that point I realized that was my body's way of telling me I wasn't all right. My mom was in the other room, but my brother was sitting right beside me. I told him I was fine but he insisted on telling my mother.

My mom came to check on me and, for some reason, immediately went over to the medicine cabinet. There was really no reason for her to do that because I don't remember her ever going to it when we had an upset stomach. I chalk it up to motherly intuition. She looked through the cabinet and started taking inventory. I had forgotten how meticulous my mother was at keeping up with how much of everything we had. Looking back, I'd say she was probably an obsessive-compulsive.

164

It didn't take long for her to notice the missing packs from the Dimetap box. She didn't really miss the Tylenol because I only took a few of those and the bottle was still about half full. She sent me to my room and told me to wait up there for her. By this point, I was really sorry I hadn't died in my sleep. I knew there was going to be hell to pay.

When my mother came in the room, I was shocked at how calm she was. She patiently asked me what all I had taken, when, and why. As I laid out the details of what all I took, she realized how serious this was. The mix of pills and alcohol had obviously not been enough to kill me, but it was quite enough for her to snatch me up and take me to the emergency room.

As we were driving there, she kept asking me questions. She knew about the sexual abuse, but that was something we just didn't talk about. And this time was no different. When I mentioned it, she begrudginly acknowledged it, but quickly moved back to the actual attempt.

While I was at the hospital, they made me drink some charcoal drink to make me vomit as much as possible. After that, they pumped what was left in my stomach out. As I was in the bed in the emergency room recovering from the whole puke and pump ordeal, I could hear my mother in the next room sobbing uncontrollably. I guess she was able to maintain her composure until she knew I was going to be okay.

It was at that point I realized she wasn't the hard-ass I made her out to be. She was hard on me at times because that was her job. I believe this episode was enough to scare her into realizing that no matter what she did, I was still my own person with my own problems. As I said before, she knew about the abuse and would quickly squash and change the conversation any time the subject came up.

At the time, I thought it was because she didn't care about me or didn't really believe it happened like I said it did. That wasn't the truth at all. I think she never wanted to talk about it because she saw it as her fault on some level because it was her job to protect me and she failed miserably in that case. Despite her lack of willingness to talk about my problems, she and my dad agreed to send me to therapy after that.

Thankfully, it was the therapist's job to listen to me in a non-judgemental, compassionate manner. Finally, someone was willing to believe me unconditionally.

My advice to anyone with a child going through behavioral issues, whether it's founded in sexual abuse or just a lack of friends, is to teach that child self-confidence and self-esteem. It's so easy to discount the feelings and opinions of a child just because they are young. That doesn't make their problems, however minor it appears to an adult, any less important to them. In fact, an issue that would seem minor to an adult is a major deal to a child.

Remember how hurt you felt as a child if someone called you ugly or stupid? Everything they experience is

new and exciting and overwhelming. Don't forget that.
Let them know that life can be hard at times, but never too
hard that suicide is the answer. Life is worth living.

18

Sexually Abused Child Part II

Well, I told you about my brush with suicide at age twelve. This is the story of my attempt at age twenty-one. From the time I was twelve, up until this attempt, I saw a laundry list of therapists and dealt with depression off and on. When I was in high school I developed an eating disorder (bulimia). This was in response to the highly competitive culture of teenage girls in my school in their pursuit of the "it" guy.

Even though I felt this mentality was childish and short-sighted, I still succumbed to the drive to look sexy. That pretty much sums up my high school years—binge, purge, therapy, repeat.

It wasn't until after I graduated from high school that I found my "happy place." On a whim, I took a trip to South America. I'm not sure what prompted me to do it. Maybe it was just my desire to get away from everything I knew and immerse myself in something completely foreign. Well, it worked. My time down there was so therapeutic. I went through such an invigorating and de-stressing period, when I returned home, no one could believe I was the same person. It was like a re-birth.

When I started college, I was known as the "smiley kid" on campus. People would actually ask me why I smiled so much or why I was so happy. Even my family made a point of mentioning how happy I seemed to be.

My first semester of college was nothing short of spectacular. I was in a new place, on my own, away from home. It was like a dream come true. My roommate was somewhat annoying, but I didn't let her negativity bring me down. But as the year went on, I noticed I wasn't smiling as often. Near the end of the second semester, people had quit commenting on my smile.

As it turned out, that trip to South America was a refreshing change of scenery, but it wasn't the life-altering experience I had played it up to be in my mind. Sure, the effects were genuine, but they were not as long-lasting as I had hoped they would be. The same was true for my college experience. Initially, it was so wonderful because I had moved out of my parents' house into my own place (with a roommate). After the newness had worn off, I realized it was just an extension of my home and my problems were still with me. I was not able to leave them at home.

As the first year went on, I started getting more and more annoyed by my roommate. The things that I was able to ignore in the beginning were now so annoying I wanted to slap her everytime I saw her. For a while, I was able to avoid her because I knew her schedule as well as I did my own. In time, though, our paths inevitably had to cross. Although I considered myself a strong person, looking back, I realize that I tended to let people walk all over me. That was most likely the root of my anger toward my roommate. I let her run all over me and I was really mad at myself for letting her do so.

The next year was nothing to speak of. It was more of the same, but nothing out of the ordinary. My junior year I decided to find another roommate. In the hopes of finding someone I could room with without any drama, I randomly picked a "roommate wanted" ad off the bulletin board in the student union.

At first she seemed to be a perfect fit for me. She kept to herself and tended to leave me alone. About a month into it, though, she began to take more interest in what I was doing. It was innocent at first, but with time it became obsessive.

She seemed to really care about my opinion. In the beginning, it was flattering, but eventually she became so needy that she wouldn't do anything without first asking me what I thought. By this time, I had a boyfriend that I was getting pretty serious with. I didn't have time to be babysitting a roommate with an inferiority complex.

I started spending more and more time with my boyfriend. I had convinced myself it was because I loved him so much, but I think a big part of it was so I could stay away from my roommate. This constant time together proved to be a little too much for my boyfriend. He started giving me signals that he wasn't as serious about our relationship as I was. A big part of that was him spending more and more time with his friends instead of me. I had friends of my own, but they were really more like acquaintances, so I didn't really hang out with them. By this time, I had halfway moved in with him even though I was still paying rent on my own apartment. He'd go out with his friends and leave me at his place all alone. Several times he wouldn't come in until after I had gone to sleep.

The more time I spent alone, the more those old feelings of low self-esteem and worthlessness began to creep back in. Depression was like a cloud in the distance I could see coming my way. I knew it was coming for me and that I needed to run from it as fast as I could. The problem is, depression is not something you can simply run from. It will keep pursuing you until you're too tired to run any more.

Eventually, it caught up to me and I was totally engulfed by it. I was completely lethargic, like I was in a deep hole that I could not climb out of. It was the kind of depression that makes you feel alone, even in the middle of a crowded room. It got so bad that from time to time I would hear thumping in my ears. At first, I thought our neighbors would just be playing their music too loud. I'd bang on the wall but would not get an answer. Then I would put my ear to the wall only to realize there was no

171

music playing on the other side. That's when I knew I needed to seek help.

Since I was in college, I had not had any counseling. A big part of that was because of my South American "re-birth." However, I recognized what was happening and sought help through the free on-campus counseling center. This was the first time I got put on medication for my depression. During this time, my boyfriend officially broke up with me. It had been a long time coming, he just stated the obvious. This didn't help things at all. I felt alone again, in all senses of the word.

It was at this point I met a girl who was going through a lot of the same struggles as me. I didn't realize at the time that befriending someone just as screwed up as you is a terrible idea. We had very deep, macabre conversations that involved all the various ways we would kill ourself if and when we decided to do it. It was fun to a point, but it was really twisted after a while. At the time, I was thankful to have someone that understood me and didn't criticize or condemn me for my thoughts or feelings. In reality, it was a very unhealthy, co-dependent relationship.

After one of our suicide planning sessions, I decided I was going to see my old boyfriend. I called him to let him know I was coming over. He was less than thrilled but agreed nonetheless. For some reason, I still longed for his approval. When I got there, he seemed unhappy to see me and basically just tolerated my presence. He ignored me half the time and paid very little attention to me the rest of it. What little shred of hope I had of him wanting me back

172

was quickly deflated. It was at that point I told him I was planning on hurting myself. He thought I was bluffing and just blew me off. Seeing that I was getting nowhere, I left.

As I was driving back to my apartment, I was consumed with the thought of ending it all. Throughout this internal struggle, my hands ached mercilessly from the intense grip I kept on the steering wheel. It was only by sheer determination I made it back to my place.

It was at that point I called my mother and told her about what happened with my ex. I told her not to worry though, that I wasn't going to hurt myself. Since I had attempted suicide at age twelve, I was hoping that she caught that as a cry for help. Unfortunately, she seemed to be barely paying attention and said, "oh, okay honey." That was the last obstacle that was going to prevent me from killing myself.

I sat down on the couch and wrote out several letters. They were to my parents, my siblings, my (few) friends, and, of course, my ex-boyfriend. I wanted them all to know how much I was suffering and how each and every one of them missed their chance to save me.

My roommate had a prescription for codeine. I went through her dresser drawers and found it. The bottle was almost full, but I only took sixteen or seventeen pills.

This was such a cry for help more than a legitimate suicide attempt because, if I had really wanted to kill myself, I would have taken the whole bottle. In my mind, I was trying to take just enough to kill myself. I grabbed a bottle of Southern Comfort and used it to wash down the codeine pills. Again, I drank just enough to take the pills, no more. With that, I went to bed.

A couple of my friends called me that night because they had heard I went to see my ex-boyfriend and wanted to check on me. I convinced them I was fine, so they didn't come over. However, the next morning when I didn't show up for work, they immediately came to my apartment. They were relieved to find me alive. Their relief was short-lived when I told them what I had done. They insisted I let them take me to the hospital.

After a few minutes of trying to convince them I was okay, I could tell they weren't letting up. So, I agreed to go with them to the hospital. After I went through the whole rigmarole of getting my stomach pumped and the whole nine yards, my friends made me call my parents to let them know what I had done. It was at that point my mom realized the call I had made to her the night before was a cry for help.

She was so disappointed in herself for not catching it. I told her it was okay. She and my dad drove up the next day and took me out of college. One of the biggest frustrations I have with myself is that I was only a year away from finishing college, but I never went back.

Since those times, I have come to realize I should not look to others for my own self-worth. I have learned I must go inward for the most honest and the most relevant answers for me and my current situation. Some of the techniques I use are meditation, yoga, and acupuncture. Also, I am more likely to let my loved ones know when

I'm hurting. I don't sugarcoat it or hint around, I come right out and tell them. My days of being subtle and timid are over.

I've come to recognize when that cloud of depression is creeping up on me and I quickly make it known. I also know those times at twelve and at twenty-one when I attempted suicide were not spur-of-the-moment things. Each time, it was at least six or more months in the making.

When you're talking with someone who's suicidal, you must realize they most likely have considered it for a while. And you can "talk them off the ledge" this time, but that's not the end of it. If it took them months to get the courage to try or almost try it, one pep talk sure as hell isn't going cure them! Keep in touch with them after that. You showed them you cared enough to stop them from suicide. Don't walk away thinking that's the end of it.

To those who are hurting, stop searching for answers or approval from others. Be proactive about going inward (in a spiritual sense). If you go to a therapist, find one that you "click" with. I've been to enough to know that if you don't have a therapist you feel you truly connect with, you'll end up going in circles and feel like you've basically accomplished nothing. Most of all, share with those you love how much you are hurting. Believe me, they want to help you, but chances are they have no idea how much love and support you really need. Tell them.

19

Spina Bifida

There are various challenges you encounter when dealing with a birth defect like spina bifida. First of all, neither the town nor the times in which I was born were the most "handicap-friendly." It was decades before all the laws and regulations were passed to make things a little easier and more accessible for people like me. And when you're young, you hate your disability.

But, as you get older, you learn to accept it and make lemonade out of lemons, so to speak. However, when you get even older (especially mid-life), you hate it again. And from there it only gets worse. I was not cut out for the role of "the little cripple that could."

As you can imagine, in school I got teased quite a bit for being "different," especially since I was the only one in school with a disability. Kids can be cruel, you know. Looking back, though, they didn't know any better. They were just ignorant and were, I'm sure, parroting what they overheard at home. They say that what doesn't kill you makes you stronger. Not always.

As I progressed through school, the taunts got a lot more vulgar and definitely more cruel. The difference at that point was I had a few close friends who were more than willing to step up and fight for me (literally). They didn't make me feel like I was a charity case; I was their genuine friend. I guess their physical protection gave me a sense of security and boosted my self esteem a bit because it was around that time that I really started developing a wicked wit. So, whenever a knucklehead wanted to pick on me and try to seem tough for his buddies, I was able to embarrass the shit out of him instead. Plus, I knew that if my wit wasn't enough, my buddies would kick his ass! It's hard to believe that looking back, high school was probably the best time of my life. Kinda funny based on how awful my first few years of school were.

Fast forward to the not so distant past. Before companies were required to be "handicap friendly," there weren't a whole lot of options for someone with a physical disability such as mine.

So, I ended up doing office work for the nearby police department. It wasn't my dream job, but it was work. It worked out well because whenever they needed someone to work nights, weekends, or holidays or to cover someone else's shift, I was usually available to fill in. I mean, what else would I have going on?

As the weeks turned into months and then years, depression really started getting a grip on me. I felt stuck in a dead end job that I was made to feel appreciative to have because, what else could a cripple do for a living anyway? Police departments, at least back then, were kind of an "old boys' club." Either you ran with 'em or you didn't. There was no middle ground. And because I didn't move around with the greatest of ease and I required special accomodations when I traveled, I tended to be left out of "boys' night out" most of the time. I tried to comfort myself by saying I was more important to them by staying at work and being the "go-to guy." The only person buying that load of crap was me (and I wasn't too convinced either).

It was around that time in my life when I was first diagnosed with clinical depression. Less than a year later, I took an extended leave of absence for mental disability. That didn't help my ego very much. Now I had mental and physical disabilities. Good God! How much worse could my life get? Here's a bit of advice, never, never, never ask yourself that question because it is like a voodoo kiss of death that seems to attract even more bad luck and heartache into your life.

Let me say this, through most of my life, I have tried to be honest with myself. I know it couldn't have been easy for my parents to raise a disabled child, especially in the 1950s and the 1960s when the world was a lot less friendly to people with disabilities. They deserve nothing less than sainthood, if you ask me.

When I got married, I thought I had found someone who cared for me as much as my parents did. She saw the "inner beauty" that I possessed. Even though I felt like a burden most of the time (as I did with my parents), she never seemed to complain too much, outside the grumpiness of being exhausted. Lord knows, I didn't blame her for that. We seemed to have a really good thing going ("seemed" being the operative word).

Was I ever wrong. After several years of marriage, she informs me we're getting divorced. What, what, what? Where the hell did this come from? I was dead set against it, but she was 100 percent determined to go forward. In the divorce papers drawn up by her lawyer she listed the reason for the divorce as "irreconcilable differences."

How could we reconcile our differences if I didn't even know what they were? I know I'm not the most simple guy to get along with, but who is? It's not like she married me thinking I would someday become un-cripple. This was a total shock and a major blow to my ego. How could things get any worse? I'm sorry I asked.

For years, I had floated in and out of the depths of depression, but this sent me on an express elevator all the way to the basement. All the taunts and slurs from my childhood began haunting me in my dreams. A night barely went by that I didn't wake myself up crying or screaming obsenities at childhood bullies. I felt sorry for myself and felt like no one cared about me anymore. I was no count and had no business even being here on earth. The pity party was in full effect.

While the divorce was being finalized, I had nowhere to go. So I moved back in with my parents, temporarily. Well, temporarily has become something more like semi-permanently. My folks live away from any kind of bustling metropolis to say the least. None of my friends live very close and I have no transportation. Here's a recipe for disaster: a middle-aged man with clinical depression, confined to a wheelchair, in the midst of a divorce, living with his parents, with no nearby friends, and a lot of time on his hands. It was only a matter of time because I hit the iceberg.

At this point, I had made up my mind and, after a little research, I had planned out how I was going to kill myself. With all the thought I put into this, the date was the most random of it all. Basically, I looked at the calendar and picked a date. It was two weeks away. My choice for my sweet angel of death? Pain pills, and lots of them.

Two weeks would give me enough time to save up enough to get the job done. I cut back on what I normally took each day to what I absolutely needed to get by each day. It ended up being nearly a double fistful of OxyContin (about 50 total). And in the remote chance that those weren't enough to get the job done, I had my trusty pistol on my nightstand. Needless to say, I was determined.

As far as a note goes, I wasn't going to leave one because, honestly, I didn't care to say goodbye to anyone. I felt I had been such a burden my entire life that I wouldn't even be missed anyway. This would lessen the strain and the extra responsibilities I had placed on my aging parents as well. It wasn't fair to them to have to take care of me all over again. Raising me once was enough. A note was not really necessary anyway, because the few people closest to me would have figured it out pretty quickly.

I was two days away from doing it when the oddest thing happened. I started getting friend requests on Facebook. A few weeks prior, I had opened an account as a fluke but had pretty much forgotten about it. As corny as it may sound, all of a sudden I felt cared for. I was getting requests from people I hadn't seen or heard from in ages; some all the way back to grammar school. Was this dumb luck or divine intervention?

This was enough to sidetrack me for a few days. I missed my initial "target date," but I was still determined to do it, by God. One of my recently acquired Facebook friends called me. Even though we only lived about 30 minutes apart, I hadn't talked to her in months, if not years. We must've talked for three hours. I ended up confessing to her my plans for suicide. Let me rephrase that. I told her I had thoughts of suicide, but didn't tell her I had planned it out with an exact method and a date.

There wasn't any one thing she said that "snapped me out of it." She just did a great job of cheering me up and encouraging me to hang in there a little while longer. Essentially, she lowered a ladder into that deep hole of

181

depression I was still living in. Now it was up to me whether or not I would climb out.

Since then, I have slowly crawled out of that hole. Occassionally, I will slip a little, but not to the depths where I once was. I have learned how to cope with my thoughts and emotions. I have also learned that I am capable of committing suicide without a second thought. I'm not saying that with any kind of boastful pride, or shame. It's just a fact.

If things ever get that bad again, I may actually go through with it. However, I feel that I've learned my lesson about isolating myself too much. With the assistance of Facebook, I don't feel so isolated. Even though I'm physcially distant from most everyone I know, I'm not emotionally so. The phone has been quite a savior as well. As my friend told me before, "you call me day or night, whenever you need to talk. Don't make me come over there and beat some sense into you!" God bless friends who love you enough to put it to you in less-than-couthful terms.

If you are considering suicide, my advice to you is this, reach out to someone, anyone. Isolating yourself is a recipe for disaster. Do not bottle things up. Keep talking to friends, strangers, anyone who'll listen. Just don't give up. If you have a friend or a family member who you suspect may be, call them, email them, visit them. Just let them know how much you care about them and how special they are to you. Everyone needs to hear that from time to time; even the meanest, crabbiest old bastard you may know.

Trusting in God and keeping regular contact with my friends (via phone, email, or Facebook) has kept me from (seriously) revisiting suicide. When I get down, I always remember my friend's advice: hang in there a little while longer.

20

Suicide by Facebook

In August 2014 Josh Gracin, an *American Idol* alumnus from Spring Hill, Tennessee, posted an ominous message on his Facebook page:

> **I've loved her for seventeen years. I made mistakes . . . I admitted them, told her the truth and she turned her back on me when I needed her help the most . . . Please remember me as someone who gave his all in his music . . . Pray for my family as they carry on in this world without me. Goodbye.**

A family member alerted police to the post and they rushed to his home, where they found Gracin's wife but not him. Later, police located the 33-year-old singer driving in the area not far from home. They escorted him to a hospital, where he was evaluated by physicians and then r21eleased. Subsequently, Gracin's manager took over his Twitter page to report: "Thank you everyone for your prayers & concern. Josh is safe & with his family now. I promise to update soon."

Gracin's note put a focus on the obvious. No one knows how many suicide notes have been posted on Facebook or Twitter, but it is clear that social media is destined to become the communication vehicle of choice for many individuals contemplating suicide.

That realization has prompted Facebook to develop a "suicide policy" for its users. In a message labeled "Report Suicide Content," Facebook said: "Important. If you've encountered a direct threat of suicide on Facebook, please contact law enforcement or a suicide hotline immediately. If the person you're worried about is a member of the U.S. military community, be sure to mention this so they can provide this person with custom support."

In a formatted message application Facebook asks for the name of the person who posted the content and a copy of the message as it appears on Facebook. They also request interested parties to copy and paste the link to the individual's post so that Facebook can investigate.

As time goes by, suicide by Facebook is likely to become a major problem, simply because it has become a primary communication vehicle for so many individuals, many of whom rely solely on the application for social intercourse—and because it provides instant recognition for the individual writing the farewell note. If the writer sticks around a few minutes he or she can determine how many "friends" "like" the post.

21

Traumatized Youth

What are the events that led up to my thoughts of suicide? My goodness, where do I start?! When I was 10 years old my dad hanged himself.

It was a seemingly normal day. My grandmother came over to our house looking for my dad. She needed him to fix something for her. Mom and I went with her outside to look around the farm.

I was the first one to make it to the barn. There, hanging from one of the rafters, was my father. With as much violence as there is on television now, it's not so hard for kids to process the image of someone hanging themself. However, back then that kind of stuff was rarely accessible to a 10 year old, especially in our household.

They said I began screaming so loudly they thought I was hurt. It's strange what memories survive from certain situations. I don't remember anything except seeing my big, strong dad dangling from the end of a rope—and that I was holding half a tuna sandwich I had been eating when we began the search.

Once my grandmother got there, she ran over to daddy and picked up on his legs to give the rope a little slack. My mom was screaming at me to run in the house and get a knife from the kitchen so she could cut him down. Honestly, I don't remember who actually went into the house to get the knife. It could have been my mom, my grandmother, or even me. I was in such shock that all I can remember doing was shoving my sandwich into the chicken coop because I didn't want it anymore.

They cut my dad down, laid him on the floor of the barn, and began vigorously shaking him and calling his name. Out of nowhere an ambulance pulled up. Looking back, either my mom or my grandmother must have gone to get the knife because I wouldn't have had the presence of mind to call the paramedics. Once they began working on daddy, he began coughing and struggling with them. They said we had found him in time, thankfully. The details after that are blurry because I was sent to stay with our neighbors for two or three days.

It turns out that Daddy is manic depressive. So many people call it bipolar. I think that's a way of trying to sugar coat what it really is. You experience two major phases, mania and depression. Bipolar sounds like some kind of vacation you take if you're a mountain climber. On top of that, he's a raging alcoholic. If that's not a volatile combination, I don't know what is.

One gift my dad did give to me was the trait of manic depressive. Fortunately, I do not have the taste for alcohol. I don't like the way it makes me feel; especially the lack of control. I love to micromanage and to be in control. Let me be the designated driver or the babysitter and I'm good to go.

That was the first major event in my life that contributed to my desire for suicide. The next thing came at age fourteen. It was at that point in my life when I was raped. I had a really hard year after that. We went to court and had that whole thing to deal with (way more than any fourteen-year-old girl should have to endure). Even worse than that is I had to continue to go to school with him and his hoodlum friends.

At school, I was getting threatened and harassed by his friends on a daily basis to drop the charges. To top it all off, the officials at the school where I went could have cared less. Don't ask, don't tell—the ostritch syndrome.

My attacker wasn't allowed to speak to me, so he had his friends do his dirty work for him. They actually grabbed one of my friends and raped her in the school bathroom just to send me a message. They tried to grab another one of my friends in town, but stopped because they were spotted by her brother and ran off.

I got the message and refused to testify, especially when I heard they were going after my sisters next (the youngest was eight at the time).

No matter the ramifications on me, I wasn't about to let them hurt my sisters, even if it meant him getting off scott free in my case. That didn't stop me from telling everyone I knew, though. I figured if I warned enough girls to stay away from him, his field of prey would be greatly reduced. He actually raped a couple of girls I had warned, but they didn't avoid him because they didn't believe me. Well, I did my part by warning them.

Worst of all, since I refused to testify, my mother believed I was making the whole thing up just to get attention. I mean, come on, your mother is the one person you should be able to go to for anything. This was one of the darkest moments in my life and my own mother didn't believe me. She would go so far as throwing it in my face from time to time. That was just another layer of callousness on my heart. After that, my mom and I barely got along at all. My dad would even say, "Well, you know how your mama is. Just leave her alone and go along with whatever." She and I would fight like cats and dogs. We literally would get into fist fights.

Now, fast forward to age seventeen. A couple of weeks before I got to the point of suicide, mom and I had gotten into a really vicious knock-down, drag-out fist fight. By this age, manic depression was really showing its symptoms in me. Looking back to when I was ten, I began to truly understand how my dad could have felt enough anger and despair to hang himself.

The dark side of manic depression had really tightened its noose on me and was deeper than I had ever experienced before. So, I packed up my shit and told mom I was leaving. She said she wasn't going to let me leave. I was having none of that; I called one of my friends to come by late one night and then sneaked out my bedroom window. He took me to his house to stay with him and his mother. We even went to church together the next day. My manic phase was in full effect. I was finally free!

When my mother heard about what had happened, she threatened to press charges on my friend and his family (for what exactly, I have no idea). That was not fair! They were just trying to help. Nonetheless, I didn't want them to get into any kind of trouble, so I had them take me back home. When I got home, oh, boy, was my mom wound up! She cussed and screamed at me six ways from Sunday. Being manic depressive, my switch flipped from super high back to rock bottom. And all my mom could do was add fuel to the fire. I was already on the edge, now my mom was pushing me off of it as hard as she could.

When my parents went to bed, I got a notebook, went in the living room, and got ready to write my suicide letter. Before I started, I went into the bathroom and got one my dad's bottles of lithium. I found one that was full and took the whole thing. Just for good measure, I found some cold pills (the little red ones, maybe sudafed) and popped out as many as there were in the blister pack and took them too. There had been no planning or research, I just figured I'd take a bunch of pills and see what happened.

I don't know if my little sister even knows this, but I was mainly writing the letter to her because I didn't want her to blame herself or feel guilty for what I was about to

190

do. But I could not stay in that house under the same roof as my mother any longer! It was just too much to bear. So, I began feverishly writing. By that time, the medicine was taking effect and had begun to numb my senses. As a result, when I turned the pages, I couldn't hear them.

They must have been pretty loud because all of a sudden my mom appeared out of nowhere in her nightgown asking me what the hell I was doing in the living room. She snatched the notebook out of my hands, began reading, and started screaming for my dad. My father ran in the room. Let me tell you, I'm a daddy's girl to this day, even at age thirty-seven, I'm still a daddy's girl. So, to see him in such a panic really got my attention. Through the hazy, drunken-like stupor I could still see the concern and the despair in his eyes. What had I done?

At this point, I could barely stand. I was propped up on our old television set. You know, the kind that looks like a piece of furniture. Back then, I had little-to-no fingernails, but I was clutching that set so hard that I left fingernail marks in it that are still visible to this day.

Although I could barely hear, I understood that my dad was asking me what kind of pills I had taken. I motioned to the empty bottle. He abruptly left the room and came back with a full bottle from the medicine cabinet. He asked how many I took and began shaking a few into his hand. This many? No. This many? No. He poured out the whole bottle.

This many?

Yes.

In what I've come to realize as the strangest turn of events in my life, my father then took all the pills he had in his hand. *What the hell, Daddy?*

He said, "Now you have to take of me."

I let go of the television to reach out to him and dropped to the floor. The pills had really taken effect on me.

The next thing I knew, I was in the hospital. My dad was, too. We both had to have our stomachs pumped. Later, I found out that after I passed out daddy had tried to vomit the pills he took but was unsuccessful. I awoke to the sound of people crying. Looking around the room, I could see various family members gathered around me.

While I was unconscious, my mother told everyone I had tried to kill myself because my boyfriend had broken up with me. She had my notebook and had read it several times, so she knew damn good and well she was the reason I wanted to kill myself. However, she wouldn't dare let anyone know the real reason was her and that our "perfect little family" was actually a fucked up bunch of misfits. By laying down her false story before I ever woke up, she knew the family would believe whatever they heard from an adult a lot quicker than they would from a love sick teenager. It was yet another way for her to avoid responsibility and to control my life.

The worst part of my suicide attempt was the effect it had on the ones I loved. To see just how bad it hurt those who truly cared about me was the most awful thing. If you've never seen a grown man cry, don't ever give them a reason. It is the most heart-wrenching thing you could ever imagine. Even my big, brawny cousin, who I thought was a heartless bastard, totally broke down in the hospital at my bedside.

So, no matter how hard things get, I will never, never, ever put them through that again. It's not fair to them and it's not fair to me either. It's just a mean thing to do, not to mention extremely selfish. I realized afterwards I am too strong a person to just give up. Too many people love me and depend on me. When any of them, even to this day, look at me with the slightest hint of pitty, it tears me up inside. I don't want any of them to ever hurt for me again.

If anything, I want to be the one that hurts for them. I care more about others than I do myself. I've always been that way. That's why when I saw how much that incident hurt the ones I loved, I was sick to my core. When I reflect upon it, even now, I get that creeping feeling in my gut like I'm going to vomit.

My advice to others is don't be so selfish. Realize from my story just how much your actions affect others, especially the ones you love. You may not think so, but it's true. I had no clue how much my friends and my family actually cared about me. I was so focused on me and how much I hated my mother that I couldn't see the countless blessings surrounding me in every direction.

I'm quick to share my story with anyone who'll listen because I want people to learn from my mistakes. Suicide is not something you do to yourself, it something you do to everyone else. That may sound like a great way to get back at others, but it's not. Care more about other people than you care about yourself.

Life's too short and too precious to live behind some cloak of deception in order to be respected by others. Being honest and candid may not always be the easiest or the most comfortable thing to do, but it's the right thing. And, in the long run, it's the most respectable too.

Lastly, if there's one person in this world, just one, who cares about you, be responsible enough to never put them through more pain than you're going through.

22

Veteran

Going to war is never easy, not for anyone. But for me, the main trouble started after I got home. Being in the line of fire is scary, of course, but when you've been trained for that type of situation, your instincts kick in. It's not until you're home safe and sound that it really sinks in what you experienced.

That's also when the nightmares began.

Like most soldiers, I was young and full of piss and vinegar. Unlike most of them, I avoided the draft by enlisting. It's not really like I had a choice, though. When I came in from working the fields, I looked in the mailbox only to find a draft notice from Uncle Sam.

As you may have figured out by now, this took place 40-plus years ago, when there was a draft for all eligible males over the age of eighteen (not females). I quickly put the envelope back in the box and immediately drove to the nearest enlistment office. If I got drafted, I knew I would most likely end up a grunt in the trenches. If I enlisted, I would at least have a fighting chance of getting something a little more desirable, if there is such a thing in war time.

As luck would have it, after joining the Air Force, I got assigned to business/clerical work because of how well I scored in that section of the entrance tests. This was after basic training, of course. So, I still had the same battle training under my belt as all the other guys. I never was much of a gun person, but I have to admit, it felt good to know I could handle one pretty well after all that training, especially if I ever got in a life or death situation. And being in the military in war time was about a 100 percent guarantee that I would see action at some point or another. After basics, I got sent to various bases around the world for a few months at each location. My number one job was payroll. I was the guy that paid all the other soldiers. I have to admit, I kind of liked my job.

Growing up poor like I did, I always looked for alternate ways of making money. Being the guy in control of all the money made me a very popular person. It didn't take long for me to realize pilots pissed their money away like water. The reason was most of them went on a mission with the idea that they very likely were not going to make it back. What did that mean for me?

Loansharking! I didn't force any of these guys to get advances on their paycheck. I just provided a service they requested. How it worked was, they'd give me something of value like a watch or a gun, and I would give them an advance on their next check. It was easy for me to find out what their next paycheck would be. When they came back, I'd return their collateral and they'd give me the money, plus interest (of course). If they didn't come back, well, let's say I ended up with a lot of jewelry before the war was over.

After getting moved around to various bases in out-of-the-way locations, I began to get lazy. By that I mean, I actually forgot there was a war going on because I was generally on the other side of the earth from it. I tended to work at refueling bases. They were typically pretty laid back and uneventful.

All that changed when I took a hopper flight and ended up with a layover at a SAC (Strategic Air Command) base. They did things by the book all day, every day. I was definitely not used to that. This reminded me way too much of basic training. I thought that was all just a bunch of rah, rah bullshit to get us fired up to kill the "enemy." I didn't kill people. I was in payroll. This is where my wartime experience got real in a hurry.

Once a bomber came in from a mission rittled with bullet and flak holes. These guys must have flown through some serious shit. Like I said, I wasn't used to so much action. Medics were running everywhere. Other soldiers were screaming at me to get out of the way.

It seemed like everywhere I stood, I was in the way of somebody. Then I saw him. A buddy of mine from New York that I had gone through basics with. He actually slept two bunks over from me.

What the fuck had happened? He was on a stretcher and was a bloody mess. I called out his name and he struggled to look my way. A strained wink and a weak attempt at a "thumbs-up" were all he could muster. I gave him a quick salute as he and the medics disappeared into the building behind me.

After things died down a little, I found one of the medics and asked him how my buddy was and if I could slip in and say hello to him. He said, "No chance, partner. Your buddy's dead. Too much blood lost before we got to him."

The war just became real.

Before, when one of the pilots didn't return to pay off their debt, it was just one of two scenarios in a business transaction. I didn't really stop to think that they were dead. Their family would never see them again. If they had children, their father would never see them graduate high school or college or get married. What had I become?! It took a friend of mine dying for me to realize that this war involved people dying every day. It didn't matter if it was "us" or "them," people were dying. After that experience, I quit my "side business" and just did what I was paid to do. Nothing more, nothing less.

One night, I pulled out my locker box and looked through all the items I had acquired on hock from the "fly boys" who never came back. Realizing the weight of how I ended up with all this stuff, I got violently sick to my stomach. These are things their family would love to have. Some of them were probably family heirlooms.

198

I didn't keep records because who in the hell keeps records of an illegal loan service? So, I had no real way of identifying where most of the items came from or which base I was even at when I got them. This is when the depression really got ahold of me. I didn't realize it at first. I just thought I was having a bad day or two. Well, that turned into a month or two. Then several months.

After another two years, the war was finally over and I went home. I still had the lingering sense of depression that had become so familiar. It was such a common feeling, I had pretty much forgotten what it was like to not be depressed. When I got home, it was not really to a hero's welcome as you see so often in the movies. Sure, my family was glad to see me, but they were mainly glad because I was another hand that was so desperately needed to work the fields.

Farming is hard work and many hands make for light work (or lighter, at least). Plus, there were other guys in the community who had just gotten back as well. They had been in the real action. I was actually embarrassed when I'd see them because they had no way of knowing how easy my wartime experience was compared to theirs. And I sure as hell wasn't going to tell them how I had actually profitted during my deployment.

In the daytime I could pretty much get around the memories of what I had done while I was overseas. At night it was a whole different story. The nightmares were horrendous. Even though I had only really seen my friend all bloody and mangled, that image haunted me virtually every night. So often, it was mixed in with images of the pilots I had done loans with.

Some nights they were on the same plane as my buddy, other nights, they were the ones shooting at his plane. Every conceivable scenario got played out in my dreams. They constantly attacked my friend because they knew how much that bothered me. That was my Achilles heel, so to speak. It got so bad that I tried to quit sleeping.

Back then, there were not all the things to keep you awake like there are now, at least not that I knew about or could find. That didn't last very long. The most I could stay up without sleeping was three days. I'm not sure what's worse, the nightmares or the hallucinations from sleep deprivation.

With sleep deprivation, I began seeing the guys from my nightmares in real life! It was like a waking nightmare. With that, I began sleeping regularly again, but I tried getting stinking drunk before I went to sleep.

My thoughts were, when I got sloppy drunk, the next day I never remembered what I had done the night before. Maybe that would work with my dreams. Didn't happen that way. It seemed to make it even worse.

The lesson was this. I needed help. I had to deal with what I had done or the nightmares would never stop. So, I started going to a shrink at the Veterans Administration Hospital. Their case load is so heavy, that I just felt like another number to them. They figured I was just another shell-shocked vet looking for a laundry list of dope to take.

So, the shrink listened to my stories about my nightmares and, suprise, surprise, put me on a bunch of pills.

Oh yeah, that was after saying, "You saw only one dead guy?!"

Wow, even the shrink thinks I'm a pussy. Nonetheless, I took the pills like he said. And boy did they work. I went from dreading sleep to looking forward to it. I slept and slept and slept some more. This was great. I could finally sleep without the nightmares.

With actions come consequences. I slept so much that days, weeks, and even months flew by. My family became like strangers to me. My friends did as well. All I cared about was going to see my new best friend (my shrink) and getting those magical "don't give a damn" pills I had grown so fond of. After a while, I was reassigned to a new shrink. He began to notice I was running out of pills way too early and was requesting more and more refills than I needed.

This is when things changed. He told me he was reducing my meds for a while because he was trying a different approach than my last doctor. I told him, no thanks, I liked the way things were. He said that was the problem. I had to face my problems, not mask them.

With the reduction in meds came the return of my friend and the nightmares. They came back fast and hard. I had forgotten how brutal they were. This was just too much. I couldn't handle all the bullshit anymore. If the doc wasn't going to give me what I needed to escape this miserable life full of nightmares, I'd handle it myself.

One thing I had held onto from my basic days was that I felt much better when I had a gun nearby. Whether I was at home, in the car, or even in the fields, I kept a gun very close at all times. On the way home from the VA after a less-than-satisfactory session with my shrink, I pulled my revolver out from under the seat. As I reached for it, I felt something else very familiar, a bottle of whiskey.

I had forgotten that was even there. It must've been stuck under there for months. Kismet! I set the revolver on the seat and pulled the bottle out. All this while I was driving eighty miles an hour.

I took the top off the bottle and threw it out the window. This was how it was going to end. I'd knock out what was left in that bottle (the better part of a fifth) and then plant a bullet in my temple. If I was lucky, the car would wreck in such a way that it would look like an accident. Sure, they'd smell alcohol, but back then drinking and driving wasn't nearly as taboo as it is now.

After I got near the bottom of the bottle I looked over and saw my buddy in the passenger seat. Yes, the one I saw at the SAC base. He was talking but I couldn't hear him. Despite that, I knew he was fussing at me. I could tell by the look on his face. He pointed at the bottle and motioned for me to throw it out the window, so I did.

Then he pointed at the pistol and shook his finger at me. I knew he was telling me not to do it. Then he pointed at the road ahead. I stood on the brakes because there was humongous animal in the road, a cow I think.

I jerked the wheel just in time to miss it but slid off the road into a small embankment. I looked over to the passenger seat and it was empty. Both my friend and the gun were gone. I'm guessing the revolver was thrown out of the car during all the commotion, but who the hell knows. And I looked around for that damned cow, but there wasn't one anywhere in sight.

The car was fine, but I wasn't. I put the car in reverse, got back on the road, and drove the remaining thirty minutes home. I drove under the speed limit and wept like a baby the entire way.

Yes, I had taken advantage of people, yes my friend was dead, yes I had a drug problem, but, no, I wasn't going to let any of those factors control me any longer.

When I got home, I found every pill bottle in the house and threw them all away. Then, I took the trash out to the burn pile and lit it. I didn't want to tempt myself and end up digging through the trash in the middle of the night because I had changed my mind. This was the first day of a long, long road to recovery.

My next VA appointment was quite different. I told the doc what I had done on the way home. Yes, I even told him about seeing my dead friend. Strangely, he didn't seem surprised or concerned. He told me it was actually quite common for soldiers to see fallen buddies in times of great despair. He said, "Soldiers are buddies through thick and thin. Just because they're dead doesn't change that."

23

Wild Child

When bad things happen to good people, it's a test. When bad things happen to bad people, it's karma. Ask anyone that knew me growing up and they'd tell you which category I fell in. Actually, I'd agree with them. I was a hell-raiser, a bad seed. You know when parents say their child fell in with the wrong crowd? Well, they meant me. I was the wrong crowd.

At eleven years old I began smoking dope and drinking. The older I got, the more I would try. There was nothing out of bounds as far as I was concerned. When John Belushi died, the mixture of drugs that killed him became known as a "Belushi ball." Hell, I figured I'd try that just to see if it would kill me too! I was known as the wildest kid in town and was proud of it.

There's no one moment that I can remember that got me on that path, but there are a lot of things that have happened throughout my life that kept me on it. When I was around thirteen, a very close friend of mine (I called him my brother) died in a horrific accident. That was the first dealings I ever had with someone close to me dying.

It was mind-boggling. I just couldn't comprehend how someone I talked to one day was gone the next, forever. It just didn't make any sense. When I had trouble dealing with a situation, I always turned to my two best friends—pot and alcohol. They never let me down and they would never leave me. That got me through my heartache and confusion every time.

Things were going pretty well for the next couple of years. Then another tragedy. A girl I was very close to came to me in a dream. She told me she had died and was going away. It was so real I woke up in a pool of sweat. My parents were shocked to see me at the kitchen table the next morning wide awake when they woke up.

I told them about my dream and they just looked at each other. I knew that look. They knew something but didn't want to say. I screamed at them, "What is it?!"

They said, "Your friend killed herself late last night. We got the call from a friend but you had already gone to bed. We didn't want to wake you."

After two years, I had finally come to grips with the horrific death of one of my closest friends and now this? That was it. What good is this life anyway? I decided then and there to kick my "recreational" habits into overdrive.

It wasn't long after that when I found myself in a deep, dark place. My mind was racing. All I could think about were my two friends who were now gone. What kind of fucked up world do we live in where two of the nicest people I know are dead?

I called the father of a friend of mine. He actually had worked with me before by way of the court system. After I had gotten into some minor scrapes with the law, he counseled me and became like a second father to me. He and my mom were friends, so he took a special interest in me.

I thought if there was anyone who could help me out, it was that guy. So I gave him a call. We talked for a little while. Basically, it was me doing all the talking. I was telling him how awful my life was, how everything sucked. He said, "Son, if you really want to kill yourself, do me a favor and wait until tomorrow morning to do it. If you don't, come by and see me."

With that I said, "Okay" and he hung up. I was totally flabbergasted. What the hell just happened? Even though I still wanted to kill myself, I didn't. How could I? I had just promised my mom's friend (and my mentor of sorts) that I wouldn't. I stared out the window for a little while longer, then went to bed.

The next day, I went over to his house, just like he had asked. When I got there, he said, "It looks like you didn't kill yourself, my boy."

I said, "No, sir, I guess not."

I asked him why he told me to wait until the next morning to kill myself. He said, "Son, it's so much easier to kill yourself at night when the demons and the boogers get after you. But in the morning, when the sun is shining and the birds are chirping and you witness God's glory in full swing, it's just damn-near impossible."

How true. This man's wisdom was limitless.

Despite this hiccup in my road to self-destruction, I slowly but surely fell back into my excessive ways. For the rest of my time in high school, I kept pushing the limit further and further. All I cared about was getting fucked up and staying there. Whatever, wherever, and however did not matter. All that mattered was I stayed blitzed out of my mind until I died.

Whether that took five years or fifty, it was of no consequence to me. College was no different. It actually allowed me to expend my narcotic pallette even further. You name it, I did it. Weed, booze, acid, cocaine, ecstacy, and the list goes on. It was heaven. I lived on cloud nine.

Then came the second greatest crash of my life. By this time, I was out of college and back home living with my parents. Another dark, lonely night staring out my bedroom window, I got it in my mind again that life was just too hard to go on. The drugs just couldn't kill enough of the pain anymore.

If I wanted the hurt to end, there was only one way. This time, I had no intentions of calling my mom's friend because I didn't want him to stop me. And I didn't want to disappoint him by promising him I wouldn't do it and end up going through with it. That would just be disrespectful. He was too good of a man for me to lie to.

This time I had more resolve. Okay, I was ready. The last time, I wasn't really sure how I was going to do it. This time, I knew. My dad had several guns. A shotgun seemed too bulky and would make one hell of a mess. So, I found his stainless steel .38 Special revolver. I went back to my bedroom and began staring out the window again. All I could hear was a ringing in my ear, like a buzzing sound. Maybe I was getting myself psyched up, I don't really know what caused it. As I stared out the window at the neighbor's house, I pulled the trigger.

Time came to a screeching halt. It's like everything around me froze in place and then started slowly coming back up to normal speed. I remember my face getting hot and flushed. It seems like I heard someone screaming. After that came the rollercoaster ride to hell. Have you ever had a horrendous nightmare you wish you could wake up from? That's where I was.

Screaming and blood and fire everywhere. All I could think was "Holy shit, get me outta here!" The next thing I knew, I woke up in my bed to the sound of my mom screaming. I looked around and saw the pistol was still in my hand. I reassured her I was okay. But, I had to admit, I wasn't really sure that was true. She stuck her hand out for the gun, so I handed it to her.

Once I did, she set it on my nightstand and then slapped the ever-loving shit out of me, then immediately hugged me. She sat on the edge of my bed and we talked for probably an hour. I told her I had actually pulled the trigger and thought I was dead. She got the gun, opened the cylinder and pulled out the cartridge that was chambered. It had a pin mark on it. It was a misfire. I really had pulled the trigger after all.

Once again, I straightened up for a little while, but old habits die hard. As time went on, my body started to give me warning signals that I needed to slow down. I started losing weight and couldn't keep it on. That was of no concern to me. I was always a little on the heavy side anyway. I was on the greatest weight loss program ever. It's amazing what you get used to and can convince youself of as normal. I had lost so much weight that I started taping towels around my mid-section, under my work shirt, so my co-workers didn't realize I was so skinny. And I didn't think that was unusual.

One day, I was at my parents' house taking a shower. No one was there when I got in the shower, but my mom had returned in the meantime. She saw my car and thought nothing of it because I would stop by from time to time. When I got out of the shower, she came to the room to check on me. As she came in, I had a towel on my head and all she could see was some skinny guy with his ribs showing in my old bedroom. I had no idea.

She ran to her room, grabbed a pistol, and came back. She screamed at me to put my hands up. That's how awful I looked. She thought I was a burglar.

When I dropped the towel and said, "Mom, it's me," she screamed again. But this time was different. It was the blood-curdling scream of pain. She actually threw the gun at me and fell to the floor and began sobbing uncontrollably.

All those years, she had known what I was doing (to some extent, at least), but this was a visualization of its effects that she could not ignore. I consoled her and told her everything was all right. I made up a story about being sick and losing a bunch of weight, but she knew better.

When I got to work, the Human Resources Manager told me I needed to go home because it was slow and they didn't need me. That kind of pissed me off because they could have told me that before I drove all the way over there. When I got home, there was a big surprise waiting for me—an intervention. My mother had called and coordinated it with the HR Manager as soon as I left for work. My parents were there along with a few of my closest co-workers.

In that short amount of time, my mom had packed a suitcase for me and had made a call to a drug rehab center out West. They gave me no choice but to go. While I was at the airport, I called a friend of mine, told him what was going on, and asked him to help me. I told him where and when my flight was going to be laying over and asked him to meet me there. He agreed. He was a hellion like me and didn't want to see me in rehab any more than I wanted to go.

When I got to the layover city, two policemen were waiting for me when I got off the plane. They said when they have a younger person like myself going to rehab, they always meet them as they de-plane and escort them to their next one.   These guys were smarter than I had anticipated.

Thirty-four days.   That's how long I was in rehab. There are holes in my memory longer than that, but I will never forget those thirty-four.   It was the most intense, emotional, and sanctifying days of my life.   Of course, I showed up with an attitude that I was going to beat the system.   Okay, my airport switch-a-roo was a bust, but that was going to be the only slip-up.

They broke me down and hard.   To get rebuilt, you first have to be completely torn down.   That's what the first few days were like.   They had me pegged from the get-go as being a toughie.   All the counselers were former addicts, so I couldn't pull the "You don't really understand where I'm coming from" argument.   They knew damn good and well where I was coming from.

A few days into it, we were in a group session when someone came in with an envelope and handed it to one of the counselors.   He said, it looks like we have your HIV test results.   They named off each person one by one as being negative (clean) for HIV.

Then they got to me.   The counselor said, "I hate to tell you this, but you tested positive for HIV."   I jumped up, kicked over my chair, and shoved a couple of people. The biggest counselor in the room, a 6'6" former college football star, picked me up and slammed me against the wall.   He said, "You ain't positive for HIV, but every time you stick a needle in your arm, that's the chance you're taking. Get it?!" They had my undivided attention from then on.

The most surprising of the treatments were the hypnosis sessions. I had never really believed in that hocus-pocus stuff, but, then again, I wasn't really given a choice. It turns out, that was the most productive part of the whole rehab experience. After a couple of sessions, it was uncovered that I had been molested at age six by some local neighborhood teenagers. They actually lived a few doors down from me most of my childhood years.

I could see one of their houses from my bedroom window. But it had been such a traumatic experience, I had completely blocked it from my memory. The crazy thing was, I had actually looked up to those guys because they were star athletes. Now, so much of my youth and my unbridled anger was making sense. Those surpressed memories drove my anger and my desire to punish myself through excessive drug and alcohol use.

During my time in rehab, I gave myself over to God. It is only through His love, grace, and mercy that I am still here today. If I could go back to those moments when I contemplated suicide, especially the time when I actually pulled the trigger, what would I tell myself? Absolutely nothing. I would not change a thing. That may sound strange, but all of those things, even the molestation, shaped me and made me who I am today.

Currently, I work in the military with severely disabled and disfigured veterans. Many of them are suicidal and tend to have substance abuse problems at some point or another. If I had not had those tough, dark nights, if I had not fought my own personal demons and boogers so late at night, if I had not actually pulled that trigger, I would not be able to help so many of them to the extent that I'm able to now. To God be the glory.

"Hang in there. It is astonishing how short a time it can take for very wonderful things to happen."
   —Frances Hodgson Burnett

Photo by Mardi Allen

Postscript
By Mardi Allen, Ph.D.

In the last few months, while working on this book, I was touched by suicide numerous times. A co-worker's teenage son took his life after a series of minor conflicts that his family assumed were typical teen issues. Ironically, his father was conducting a suicide prevention training program at the same time he was choosing death over life.

That same week our church family suffered the loss of a brilliant attorney by suicide. His professional career was in jeopardy due to some bad decisions.

During the next week we learned that a family friend took his life at age fifty-four, only days after being released from an alcohol rehabilitation program. In the few days after his release from treatment, his family was hopeful that he was finally on the way to recovery.

Just days later, I learned that a friend's 23-year-old son chose suicide to end his suffering from the ridicule of his peers for being gay. On a national level we all recently grieved the death of the talented comedian Robin Williams, a man who had wealth and success, but apparently was facing an uncertain future after a diagnosis of a disorder that has a poor prognosis.

There is no body of knowledge that provides comprehensive data on how many suicides are averted each year. Anecdotal information suggests that maybe thousands of suicides are prevented yearly when others reach out and intervene.

It is crucial that efforts are made to increase public knowledge of the basic facts about suicide, who is at risk, what events lead to suicide, and the typical emotional and behavioral challenges associated with suicide. Preventing an individual from turning to suicide is complex and hard to assess due to individual differences in needs, values, environments, and tolerance levels. Research continues to provide helpful information for public awareness campaigns to prevent suicide.

Embracing the Facts

Statistics on Suicide

There are an estimated 5 million individuals who have attempted suicide in America. You may be surprised to learn that one in every nine of us experiences serious suicidal thoughts and about 5 percent of us will actually attempt suicide in our lifetime. One attempt occurs every 40 seconds leading to about 750,000 suicide attempts each year in America. In addition, there are 2,000 to 8,000 deaths each year that are suspected to be unreported or unsubstantiated suicides.

Emergency room data reveals over 400,000 self-inflected injuries come in for treatment each year. But there are many more attempts than are reflected in numbers from the emergency rooms. Some individuals who attempt suicide are either found in time or their self-inflected injuries are not treated by medical professionals. Some simply wake up after taking handfuls of medication in an attempt to die, while others survive an unexplained car accident that is actually a foiled attempt to die. Risky behaviors and living recklessly have been described by some as their way of trying to end their life without everyone knowing it was suicide.

Females attempt suicide more often than nales than males (three to one); however, more males die from suicide than females at a rate of four male deaths to every one female death. Of course, this is often explained by the methods chosen by males and females.

Males tend to choose more lethal methods. Firearms are used most frequently, accounting for over half of all suicides. Of all other methods, hanging or suffocation is used in about 20 percent of suicides, with poisoning following closely behind at about 17 percent. These three methods together are used in over 92 percent of suicides.

The most common method of suicide for women is to ingest poison, such as an overdose of medications (around 38 percent). Falls, cutting/piercing, drowning and fire are considered common, but less frequently, used methods of death by suicide.

Each year more people die from suicide than are dying from all the armed conflicts around the world and suicide now equals the number of deaths from traffic accidents. There is more loss of lives to suicide than any other single cause except heart disease and cancer.

Consider these facts:

- Suicide is the eleventh leading cause of death in the United States.
- More people die from suicide than from homicide.
- Suicide ranks second in cause of death for college students. A young person (age 15-24) dies by suicide almost every 2 hours.
- Suicide is the third leading cause of death for individuals aged 15 to 24.
- Suicide ranks fifth in cause of death for youth (age 5-14).
- Suicide ranks eighth in cause of death for males.
- Suicide ranks nineteenth in cause of death for females.
- 73 percent of all suicides involve white males.
- 80 percent of all firearm suicide deaths involve white males.
- An elderly person dies by suicide almost every

hour and a half.

- The highest suicide rate is for white males 65 years of age and older. When categorized by gender and race, white men over 85 years rank highest.

- The highest rate for all ages combined is white males, at 17.7 per 100,000.

- For all ages combined, white males, at 17.7/100,000 have the highest rate and black females, at 1.8/100,000 have the lowest rate of suicide.

Residents in the West and South typically show a slightly higher rate of suicide than the national rate of 11.1 per 100,000, with the Midwest and Northeast falling slightly below the national rate.

Prior Attempts as a Predictor

The first year after an attempt is the most likely time for another attempt. It is estimated that during the first year, the risk is 80 times greater for women, 200 times greater for men, 200 times greater for people over age 45 years and 300 times greater for white males over 65 for another attempt. A more lethal method is typically chosen on a subsequent attempt. The risk rises exponentially with multiple attempts.

As with any behavior, rehearsal or familiarity seems to reduce the associated anxiety or fear. Individuals who have attempted suicide more quickly entertain suicide as a possible option to resolve life's problems. It is familiar territory for them. They have already crossed over those emotional barriers that usually deter most of us.

Age as a Predictor

Age is also a factor for increased risk of suicide. The oldest 20 percent of the population (age 60+) accounts for about 40 percent of suicides. The increase in risk continues to climb with age. After age 75, the rate is 3 times higher among white males, rising to 6 times higher over age 80.

According to the Centers for Disease Control, since 1999, suicide among middle-aged men has shown a dramatic 27 percent increase. Sadly two of the already largest groups of individuals who commit suicide are statistically proving to be the fastest growing segments to die by suicide. These groups include the 45–60 year old male group, followed by the elderly.

The horrible news of a self-inflicted death by suicide seems slightly more understandable in the elderly or even middle age group; but no one ever considers that a youth could be so overwhelmed with the burdens of life to consider ending it.

The sobering good news is that children and adolescents who attempt suicide fail much more often than they succeed. Sadly, within the past few years, mental health clinics have reported more than a 10 percent increase in youth being seen for threatening suicide (CDC, 2014).

Youth typically have more suicidal thoughts and gesturing rather than a well thought out sukicide plan. Results from a 2007 survey among youth, ages 15-24 years, revealed that 25 percent of them had seriously considered suicide, 17 percent reported that they had actually made a plan and 12 percent acknowledged attempting suicide within the past year. (MS Youth Prevention, 2007)

Recognizing the Signs and Symptoms

Most people who commit suicide exhibit recognizable signs and symptoms within weeks before the tragic act of suicide. Sometimes it is not until much later that family and friends collectively piece together the data revealing that the deceased might have been saved if they had been more aware.

Families and friends are often forced too late to face how dire the situation actually was. The realization that signs and symptoms were unnoticed often is accompanied by overwhelming grief and guilt. Any suicide warning sign or symptom should be taken seriously and intervention attempted. Some of the typical thoughts, feelings and behaviors associated with suicide include:

Talking or writing about death, dying and suicide.
Expressing a belief there is no reason for living.
Actually speaking about thoughts of suicide.
Making self-deprecating statements.

221

Feeling trapped with no hope of change.

Feeling so miserable, they prefer to be dead.

Extreme anxiety, agitation or anger.

Changes in usual sleep patterns.

Withdrawing from activities or people they enjoy.

Securing weapons, medication, etc. used for suicide.

Increase abuse of alcohol or other substances.

Dramatic changes in mood.

Increase in risky, reckless activities without fear.

Unusualy behavior such as giving valuables away.

Sudden reconnecting with relatives or friends.

Seeking forgiveness for past conflicts.

Joking about death or "when I'm gone".

Reasons People Choose Suicide

Individual suffering can't be minimized or ignored. It's easy to consider another's problems as not significant enough to worry about. No one can feel your pain nor absolutely know how you may be suffering. There is not a specific, finite list of reasons why individuals end their own life. For many it is not one event or one stressor, it's morea cumulative effect. For some, after a series of missteps, bad decisions along with mental health problems, suicidal thoughts seem to be the only option left. This deadly option meets the individual's goal of ending the pain, stopping the shame and freeing everyone else from sharing their misery.

As more and more middle-aged white men are making choices that devastate those left behind, a growing number have left messages that indicate their feeling of shame, guilt and remorse for a life unfulfilled. At the time of their death they are convinced that no one comprehends their agony and pain. They feel they have disappointed themselves and their family. In some cases they have distorted views that their action will be a welcome relief for those who love them and they will consider their act as noble.

Sometimes adolescents and young adults take their own life to hurt others who have done them wrong or out of grief of a lost relationship. Others who take their own life see no way out of conflicts, broken relationships or can't face the shame of their recent actions. Adolescents who die by suicide are often victims of their own impulsive nature. They quickly resort to death to stop their emotional pain. There are even situations where youth commit suicide in an effort to be special or the center of short-lived attention among peers, even if it comes after they are dead.

At the moment of death their state of mind is not able to comprehend the error of their thoughts. Even brilliant students who feel they don't fit in take their own life. Teens and young adults who feel different from others, or who feel they don't fit in, fail to realize that once they go to college or get a job they will most likely find a peer group and hopefully feel accepted and appreciated. If only they could hold on a little longer.

Elderly people face more personal losses and deaths of loved ones, while they are suffering their own physical challenges, more and more are choosing suicide. The increase in elder suicide seems to be attributed to longer life spans, financial stressors, chronic illness and loneliness.

Typical reasons that contribute to individuals choosing death include:

- Recent death of a spouse or other loved one, including beloved pets.
- Divorce and related conflicts concerning children.
- Significant financial stress due to job loss, home foreclosure, etc.
- Home foreclosure.
- Prolonged illness or diagnosis of a terminal illness.
- Chronic physical pain.
- Abuse: physical, emotion, or sexual.
- Unresolved trauma (can't move beyond it).
- Legal problems or incarceration.
- Extreme humiliation, guilt and shame.
- Victim of bullying.
- Estranged from loved ones.
- Can't overcome alcohol or other substance abuse.
- Has brought shame to the family.
- Untreated depression or other mental health disorder.
- To escape overly strict parenting.

- To avoid others finding out about pregnancy or Aids.
- Anger or revenge.
- To show a boyfriend/girlfriend how much their breakup hurt.
- To carry out a suicidal pact.
- To avoid situations they feel are unbearable.
- To help the family financially through life insurance.

Mental Health Challenges That Contribute to Suicide

In addition to basic demographics there are other clear indicators of high risk for suicide. One of thestrongest predictors of being at risk for suicide is mental illness, particularly if untreated or if treatment is ineffective. A person who is under mental health care for suicidal thoughts or attempts most likely will be diagnosed with depression.

Untreated depression is considered the number one cause of suicide. Depression combined with alcohol is a lethal combination. Alcohol and other substances can quicklyincrease sadness, anger or negative effect and encourage impulsive, sometimes fatal actions. They are not capable of seeing life rationally or using wisdom to make decisions. They feel that no one will ever comprehend their pain and therefore believe the world will be better without them.

Once an individual 's thought process has fallen jinto a deep into a depression abyss it is difficult for them to use their rational mind. Their distorted thoughts and feelings are responsible for driving them toward suicidal behavior rather than seeking healthy behavior. The distortions are rooted in layers of emotional pain, loneliness and unbearable hopelessness.

There are reliable reports that Princess Diana was suicidal off and on throughout her lifetime. For many it's incomprehensible that someone as rich, beautiful and famous as Princess Di could possibly be suicidal. Depression and other mental health problems are not restricted to a certain class of people, race or gender. All of us are vulnerable given the right conditions, genetic makeup and timing. In reviewing Princess Diana's life it's clear that she suffered from anxiety, depression, had emotional turmoil as a child, and had little self-confidence.

When she married Prince Charles she felt she had never accomplished anything on her own. She was self-critical and found minimal support within the walls of the castle and that made her past insecurioties and pain re-emerge. There were documented episodes of an eating disorder and suicidal gesturing. She clearly made some poor choices to deal with her misery but as we know she sadly ran out of time to conquer her personal demons.

Depression

Many people don't really know when depression is severe enough to seek treatment. After suffering a loss of some kind, such as a job, a relationship, a death in the family or other events that happen to most of us during a lifetime, we feel sad for a while. This is considered normal; it's expected. Those typical short-term feelings of sadness or emptiness are not diagnosed as depression as long as there is a sense of recovery.

It's when that sadness continues with no relief beyond what is typical, somewhere around two weeks, or when the sadness becomes more pervasive and interferes with day-to-day activities that red flags are raised. A diagnosis of depression is made when an individual suffers from a constellation of symptoms over a prolonged period of time.

Depression often starts with a specific event in one's environment that initially creates the feelings of sadness but it doesn't always have to start that way. Sometimes it's a series of small events or long term stress or due to changes in hormones such as related to a seemingly joyous event of having a baby.

Depression is a chemical imbalance in the brain, similar to other diseases that affect our body. These chemical imbalances make the depressed individual have difficulty concentrating, feeling lethargic (no energy), and usually experiencing sleep problems and eating problems. Other symptoms may include feelings of hopelessness, helplessness, pessimism, guilt and/or anger. They may withdraw and often turn to alcohol and pain and sleeping pills to self-medicate.

A depressed individual often has much more difficulty making decisions they once could have made with ease. They may cry frequently and even neglect their personal hygiene and appearance.

No one can just snap out of it. They can't just wish themselves to happiness. Depression is a brain disorder and often an individual will spiral farther and farther down without proper treatment. Often the depression is accompanied by anxiety, making treatment more difficult. The neurotransmitters in the brain usually need assistance in the form of specific antidepressant medication and sometimes antianxiety medication to recover from the biological responses to whatever stressor, specific events or dysfunctional thoughts and feelings they experienced early in the depression cycle.

Research evidence supports the combination of talk therapy and medication for the best recovery from depression. Antidepressant medication can change the function of brain neurotransmitters, while talk therapy can help a depressed individual learn coping skills. By understanding that our thoughts and feelings dictate our behavior, a person can learn ways to change their thoughts and feelings which will affect behaviors including making wise decisions in the future.

Bipolar Disorder

Until the last decade or so, this disorder was called Manic Depression, which clearly defines the diagnosis. Bipolar, as it is now called, identifies the two opposite behavioral dimensions of the diagnosis. Bipolar is considered a high-risk diagnosis for suicide with a reported 25 to 50 percent of people who have Bipolar Disorder attempting suicide during their lifetime.

Just like Depression, Bipolar Disorder is a brain disorder connected to brain chemistry or the neurotransmitters in the brain. This brain dysfunction causes mood swings or episodes of depression and mania and creates tremendous stress on the individual and their day to day life.

Friends and family members often see the symptoms more quickly than the individual affected. Early diagnosis and treatment of Bipolar Disorder offers the best outcomes. Bipolar disorder is treatable; so seeking medical consultation, along with psychotherapy, should be considered a priority.

As mentioned, Bipolar consists of vacillations between the two behavioral dimensions. Symptoms of mania (manic behaviors) include the individual feeling a sense of euphoria and being very active, with an overabundance of energy. They sometimes feel on top of the world. They seem fearless and, as the symptoms escalate, they may be unable to process ideas that are bombarding them from every direction. These racing thoughts, restlessness, and exhilaration often lead to poor concentration and little or no sleep. They often become extremely irritated to the point of agitation and can become aggressive.

During manic episodes families can be torn apart by the irrational and irresponsible behaviors that are common for individuals who have Bipolar Disorder. Families typically describe an increase in sexual behavior, spending money far beyond their budget, abusing alcohol and other substances. Early identification and treatment is vital in helping the individual and their identified support systems make sound decisions as to how to deal with the symptoms prior to an episode. The individual usually denies that anything is wrong in the midst of a manic episode.

Not all individuals with Bipolar Disorder will exhibit all the symptoms during every episode. To meet the criteria that a manic episode exists, an individual must have at least three of the typical symptoms for most of the day, for almost every day, for a week or longer. It is easy to understand how an individual is high risk for death by their own hand, intentionally and unintentionally, during a manic episode, especially if substances are being used.

On the other end of the Bipolar Disorder is depression. The symptoms are basically the same as for individuals who are diagnosed with depression without mania, other than the depression is episodic. As with the above described depression diagnosis, an individual who is having a depressive episode feels intense sadness, usually suffers from eating and sleeping disturbances, is lethargic and can't concentrate. For a diagnosis of depression, symptoms must persist for at least two weeks. The individual describes feelings of low self-worth, hopelessness, helplessness and guilt and shame. Their pessimism about the future, anger and withdrawal from others contribute to an increased risk of suicide.

The treatment of Bipolar Disorder is often difficult and many patients are not compliant with treatment. Mood stabilizing medications are usually prescribed to treat Bipolar Disorder. During symptom-free time between episodes, many individuals begin feeling that medication is not necessary and they stop taking it. Bipolar is a long-term illness and there is no cure at this time, but management of the disorder is possible with treatment.

Most of us like to feel creative and energetic, as do individuals with Bipolar Disorder. For that reason, it can be difficult to make a case to them for treating their mania, a feeling that they often enjoy and don't want to give up. They prefer the euphoria of mania to the darkness of depression. In both states many individuals are not able to think clearly or make rational decisions.

Some individuals with Bipolar Disorder do not experience extreme manic symptoms. They simply vacillate between depression and minor symptom of mania, similar to just feeling really good. This is known as hypomania. This presentation of disorder is Bipolar II; whereas in Bipolar I there are more extreme mood swings.

It should be noted that individuals with either type of Bipolar Disorder often develop severe manic or depressive episodes and may even experience psychosis. Alcohol and other substances are often lethal when combined with Bipolar Disorder. For others, the constant turmoil of their life is too much to bear and suicide is an out.

Post-Traumatic Stress Disorder

A person who has been exposed to or witnessed a life-threatening event that results in the individual feeling intense emotional responses associated with the conscious and unconscious memories of the event may be diagnosed with Post Traumatic Stress Disorder (PTSD).

Symptoms of PTSD are usually apparent within three months after the event, but for some, symptoms are not evidenced for several years afterwards. Rape, child abuse, domestic violence, natural disasters, witnessing a death, terrorism, fire, severe accidents and military combat are some of the common experiences that cause individuals to develop PTSD. First responders, law enforcement officers and others who are frequently exposed to details of horrible events can also develop PTSD.

The emotional responses associated with PTSD often hinder an individual's ability to carry out their personal responsibilities. A person suffering from PTSD may feel shame due to their difficulty in moving past the trauma. They may become increasingly anxious and hyper-vigilant about their surroundings and may avoid any slight reminder of the event for fear of flashbacks and the associated prolonged psychological distress. These bouts can lead to significant changes in an individual's personality, social interactions and mood.

It can be difficult for family and friends to comprehend the turmoil the individual may be experiencing. Often relationships are destroyed, causing negative behaviors to escalate. Alcohol and other substances sometimes become their treatment of choice rather than working with mental health providers.

The risk of suicide increases as the individual feels a sense of loss of control over life. PTSD is treatable, but adherence to medication and psychotherapy, along with prolonged exposure therapy or another intervention can be challenging for many. Far too many military veterans have returned to shattered relationships and no job while struggling with intrusive memories of war (PTSD). The Pentagon reports that one active duty personnel dies each day by suicide, many of whom suffer from PTSD.

Psychosis

Individuals who experience psychosis have lost some contact with reality affecting thoughts, emotions and behaviors. Thoughts that include false beliefs are called delusions. These beliefs of special messages or beliefs of persecution may appear rather odd or ridiculous to others, but are very real to the individual. During psychosis, auditory hallucinations are common. The individual may be oblivious to things going on around them and their responses to interactions are inappropriate and often described as bizarre.

Psychosis usually occurs in episodes that can vary widely in length. During such episodes severe effects are

233

evidenced in the individual's relationships, work, social activities and personal care. Typically, there are only a few mental disorders in which psychotic episodes are likely to occur. Schizophrenia is the most common mental illness associated with psychosis.

Other disorders that sometimes include psychosis are bipolar, depression, schizoaffective disorder and delirium. Substance abuse can also precipitate psychosis. The onset of schizophrenia usually occurs between middle teens to 25 years of age, usually affecting more males. Schizophrenia is relatively rare, affecting close to 1.5 million Americans each year. Many individuals who live with this disorder are often depressed, feeling both hopeless and helpless about having a meaningful life; therefore the risk of suicide is heightened.

Alcohol and other substance abuse

Many people consume alcohol with little or no consequences, but for some the effects of alcohol and/or substances are deadly. Individuals who turn to substances to numb their feelings, relieve anxiety or gain confidence are deceived into thinking it's helpful.

With time, substances have to be increased to maintain the same desired effect, resulting in increased dependency, and then abuse. Long term use of alcohol affects physical, social and psychological health. Alcohol is often the first of many substances a person uses. Individuals who already are suffering from anxiety, depression, or serious health problems often misuse alcohol.

All of the mental health issues described in this chapter are always made worse by substance abuse. Often confused and desperate, individuals turn to substances to self-medicate; usually with devastating results. There is no fast rule about how much any individual can drink without adverse effects. Individual metabolisms play a huge role, but the general rule is that men who drink more than four drinks per occasion or about 14 per week and women who drink more than three drinks per occasion or more than seven per week are at risk for problem drinking.

Screening for alcohol problems typically involves an assessment of whether the person has been feeling guilty about drinking, having others mention how much one is drinking, failing to carry out responsibilities, or drinking in the morning. Many individuals turn to alcohol or other powerful substances to gain false courage to carry out a suicide plan.

Effects of Suicide on Others

If you suspect someone is considering suicide, you must understand that they are significantly affecting at least six other people. Considering the number of suicides within the past 30 to 40 years it is estimated that one in 64 Americans has been intimately affected by a suicide, but most all Americans will be touched by suicide. Suicide is a major public health problem..

In the book *Melissa*, Dr. Page describes his efforts to move on in life without his daughter. As a pastor he had dealt with death many times. He often used scripture and spirituality to carry his parishioners through their pain, but as a father he had to dig deep to find the strength to believe he could carry on as a pastor, husband and father to his other daughter.

The huge hole in his heart will never fully heal. He will always have two daughters, one in heaven and one still on earth. As a father who has grieved the fatal decision his daughter made, he suggests quietness, reflection and meditation as the most healing for those intimately affected by suicide. He advises to never let go of the good times, remember their smile, and reflect on the many firsts that were shared. And he suggests you work to live a full and meaningful life, although you will always have a wounded heart.

Through meditation, relaxation, therapy, membership in a support group and reaching out to others by education and training have all been reported as helpful in dealing with the pain of losing a loved one from suicide.

The healing process is usually very slow with many setbacks. Holidays, special occasions, memorable places or events can be painful for those left behind. Some have extreme anger at the person who chooses death leaving them to deal with life without them. Because suicide shatters the lives of many, prevention can save not only the person considering suicide, it can spare their family and friends considerable stress and grief.

The choice of suicide takes twice as many lives as homicide. Yet, it has the potential to be preventable. Early intervention is always best. Not every suicide can be prevented, but many can be if we understand the risks and know how to intervene.

If You Suspect Someone to be at Risk

We all live hurried lives. Sometimes we don't stop and look at those around us and evaluate what might be happening. If you suspect someone may be having thoughts of suicide or you see that their life has been in chaos or they are suffering from depression or other mental health problems there are simple ways to intervene and may save a life.

Do not hesitate to ask him if he is having thoughts of suicide. Asking the questions will not give them the idea or make them feel you are offering suicide as an option for their current problems. It is difficult to ask someone if they are considering suicide, but it is important to ask the question, not hint about it, or skirt around it hoping they will just tell you.

Calmly ask them if they are considering suicide; they will simply answer your question. If they are thinking about suicide and acknowledge it, they are usually overwhelmed with relief that someone actually understood their pain. If they are not considering suicide, you have not offended them by acknowledging their pain. They will appreciate your concern and probably share what is happening in their life with you.

Ask the suicide question first and if they are not considering suicide or seem ambiguous about life, inquire further about a plan. Firearms are, by far, the most common method for suicide (55 percent of all suicides are completed with a firearm), so it imperative that a suicidal person not have access to a firearm.

Hanging or suffocation is used in about one out of five suicides, which is why you can never leave an acutely suicidal person alone for a second. People who have died by hanging have used virtually every conceivable thing to hang themselves with, including shoe laces, electric cords, belts, bedding, etc. Any plan must be dismantled.

Let the individual know that you will help them through this crisis. You may need to stay with them, call in other support, call 911, or take them to see a professional. We must all take suicidal thoughts, gesturing and attempts seriously. Assist the individual in finding a reason to live. Even the seemingly smallest reason can save a life. Ask about what is important in their life—a spouse, friend, parent, pet, job or hobby.

If the individual will just hold on for another day, maybe two, even commit to waiting a week, most of the time the thoughts of suicide are diminished and they seem to find at least a little hope. Numerous studies on people who have attempted suicide indicate that they primarily want their pain to stop and ending their life seems the only option left. With intervention and proper treatment most individuals who experience suicidal thoughts can find hope and learn coping skills. Medication is often needed to address depression and other psychiatric diagnoses associated with skuicide.

There are resources and support groups in every large city and even in rural areas through the state mental health department. Mental health advocacy groups also want to help anyone who is considering suicide.

If You Are Thinking About Suicide

During tumultuous times, a fleeting thought of suicide, is not considered abnormal, but if you dwell on suicide or begin considering it as a viable option, please believe:

Help is available, no matter how severe your emotional pain might be and there are people who truly care about you and want to help.

Sharing your feeling with someone is a positive step in choosing life.

You are worthy of love and understanding.

There are times in life when emotionally distorted thinking can cloud thoughts. Suicide robs you the opportunity to reach a better state.

Untreated depression combined with substance use is the number one culprit of suicide. With professional treatment and time you will get better.

Suicide never makes things right. No situation or pain is justification for suicide.

Your family, friends, relatives and co-workers will not be better off if you end your life. Suicide is never a solution; it would only shift your pain to others.

If you choose suicide it will cause excruciating pain for those you love.

You are not weak for considering suicide and there is no shame in acknowledging your pain. You are definitively not alone in feeling hopeless.

Saying no to suicide and choosing life is possible for you. You cannot solve problems when you are dead. You cannot find happiness, change situations or contribute to others when you are dead. You cannot be an example of accepting the consequences of your decisions and learning from your mistakes when you are dead. Only in life can you make things better.

Resources and Support Groups

There are resources and support groups in every large city and even in rural areas through local mental health systems. Mental health advocacy groups also want to help anyone who is considering suicide.

Contacting the mental health authority in your area or searching the Internet can help you find resources.

If you are having suicidal thoughts call:

911
1-800-SUICIDE (1-800-784-2433)
1-800-273-TALK (1800-237-8255)
text telephone: 1-800-799-4889)
Military veterans 1-800-273-TALK, press 1)
Spanish Speaking 1-800-273-TALK, press 2)
LGBT Youth 1-866-4-U-TREVOR

American Psychiatric Association 1-888-35-PSYCH (77924)

American Psychological Association 1-800-964-2000

Nation Suicide Prevention 1-800-273-TALK

www.suicide.org

www.cdc.gov

www.samhsa.org

 www.nimh.nih.gov

www.nationalcouncil.org

www.cfah.org

www.dmh.ms.gov

Statistical and clinical data for this book were taken from the above websites.

Books on suicide mentioned in this book:

Cracked but Not Broken by Kevin Hines (Rowman & Littlefield Publishers, 2013).

Melissa: A Father's Lessons from a Daughter's Suicide by Frank Page (B & H Books, 2013).